GETTING THE BEST FROM THIS BOOK

Who's the book for?

Better Communication Skills for Work is for anyone who wants to improve their reading, writing and spoken communication skills for work. You may be:

- in a job
- on a training scheme
- going for a promotion
- thinking of returning to work
- self-employed.

What does the book do?

It will help you to:

- cope with new paperwork
- be better at dealing with people at work
- be more confident at work
- get a qualification in Communication Skills, if that's what you want.

Why should I use the book?

You will find that most jobs involve more reading, writing and spoken communication skills than they did a few years ago. This is because of new technology, changes in the way work is organised, a greater interest in customer care and an increased emphasis on improving the quality of goods and services.

This book is an introduction to the basic communication skills needed to cope with these changes and new job demands. It will help you feel more confident when you do your job and when you are thinking about applying for new jobs or a promotion.

Can I get any help?

Finding someone to talk to about the things that you are trying to do, and who might be able to give you some advice, will really help your learning. Some of the people you could try are:

- your supervisor

- a colleague at work or your shop steward

- your training or personnel officer

- a friend or someone at home

- a basic skills or communication skills tutor at your local college. (*See below*, Where can I get my work assessed?)

How can I get a qualification?

The tasks and work-related activities in this book can be used to work towards the City and Guilds certificate in Communication Skills (C&G 3793). You can find out more about the certificate on pages 116-118. If you are interested, look at these pages now.

If you do decide to use this book to get the certificate you should contact a centre offering the certificate before you start. They will be able to give you advice about:

- the level of the certificate to take.

- collecting evidence which shows that you can use your communication skills.

Where can I get my work assessed?

Many Colleges of Further Education, Adult Education Centres and Open Learning Centres for Basic Communication Skills offer this

BETTER COMMUNICATION SKILLS FOR WORK

Melanie Kelcher

BBC Books

This book accompanies the BBC television series Work Is A 4-Letter Word, first broadcast in 1992. The series was prepared in consultation with the Continuing Education Programme Committee and ALBSU and produced by Paul Simons.

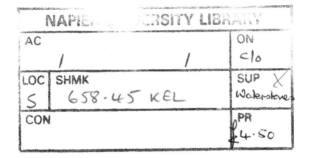
Published by BBC Books, a division of BBC Enterprises Limited, Woodlands, 80 Wood Lane, London W12 0TT.

First published 1992

© Melanie Kelcher 1992

The moral right of the author has been asserted

ISBN 0 563 36370 3

Set in Linotype Plantin by Studio 21, Windsor

Printed and bound in Great Britain by Clays Ltd, St. Ives Plc

Cover printed by Clays Ltd, St. Ives Plc

certificate (it is sometimes called WORDPOWER). To find out where you can take the certificate locally you could either:

- telephone your local college.

- telephone the national help line 0800 700 987 (you will not be charged). Give the telephone operator your name and telephone number and a basic skills tutor from your area will get in touch with you and tell you where you can go for tuition.

- ask at your local Jobcentre if there is an Open Learning Centre for Basic Skills near you. There are over 70 of these Centres in England and Wales. The Centres are well equipped with new technology so you could learn basic word processing or computer skills while you are getting help with Communication Skills. You can drop in at any time or get telephone support if you are unable to attend a Centre. You can use many of the Centres free but some do charge a small fee. Usually you will need to pay a fee to get your work assessed but do check because help is often available.

How to use this book

Each Section begins by telling you what skills can be practised as you work through it. Each Section:

- contains information and advice on five skills. This clock symbol at the beginning of each skill indicates roughly how long it will take you to read it through. For example, the clock here indicates 20 minutes reading time.

- provides short questions or tasks so that you can check yourself and practise the skills. These tasks are indicated by a pencil symbol. The number on the pencil tells you approximately how many minutes it will take you to complete the task.

- ends with some work-related activities. These are indicated by

The clocks and pencils are meant as guides only, to help you plan your time. Work at a pace that suits you best. Take a break whenever you feel like one. You can work as quickly or as slowly as you like.

Most, but not all, of the tasks and activities in this book, are linked to the certificate. $\boxed{\text{U009}}$
The symbol $\boxed{\text{E1}}$ indicates which Units and Elements of the certificate you could work towards (see page 116).

The book has been designed so that you can:

- just read and work through the bits that interest you.

- read through the whole book and complete the tasks and the work-related activities so that you can begin to work towards the Certificate. You don't need to complete all the tasks and activities although you may want to!

Some of the work-related words and phrases are highlighted in bold type. They may be new to you so they have been included in a Glossary of Terms on page 119.

There is also a list of addresses at the end of the book. You could write to any of the organisations listed, asking for further information.

Where should I start?

You could turn back to the Contents page and decide which Section of the book is most important to you now. Start at the beginning of that Section and work through it. Maybe you are particularly interested in one or two of the Sections. If so, you could start with those. If you think all the Sections are equally useful, start at the beginning and finish at the end!

Getting started

You will find studying easier if, before you start, you:

- set aside some time for studying and try to make sure you are not interrupted.

- set yourself a timetable for carrying out the tasks and activities. Remember some of them can be carried out at work.

- find someone who will help you.

- give yourself a treat when you complete an activity and finish a Section.

Then, when you start:

- read each Section through carefully before you begin any of the tasks or work-related activities.

- make a list of any new words that you find. If you are not sure of their meaning check them in a dictionary. Remember you will find the highlighted terms in the Glossary.

GOOD LUCK!

WORKING IN TEAMS

A team is a small group of people who co-operate together in such a way that they achieve more than they would if they worked alone. Many of us prefer to work in teams – we often ask friends to come with us and give us confidence when we are not sure about a situation; we club together in teams if we want to win a competition or protest about something.

If you work in a team you may find that there is less reliance on supervisors and you are responsible for managing your own work. You may be asked to become **'multi-skilled'** and be given training which will help you carry out a wider range of jobs. You are more likely to be consulted on a range of issues to do with running the business and may have regular **'team briefings'**. A successful team depends upon the co-operative skills of all the team members.

This Section will help you to:

- encourage and support other team members

- give and receive criticism

- motivate people in the team

- put across your point of view

- brief a team.

SKILL 1: ENCOURAGING AND SUPPORTING YOUR TEAM

If a team is going to be effective, each member has to encourage and support the other members. This may mean:

- encouraging others to put forward ideas.

- building and developing other people's ideas.

- creating a supportive atmosphere where people are happy to have a go, to take risks, to say what they really think.

- agreeing with something someone else has said.

It might also mean that you need to help another person solve a problem – it could be a problem associated with their home life or they may be unhappy at work.

1.1a **Choose one of the following problems:**

> Alcohol and/or drug abuse, marriage problems, mental illness, loss of home or job. Or think of a problem that you have had to deal with in the past.
>
> Make a **'contact list'** of names and addresses of organisations where you can get information and professional help.
>
> *(For help on Finding Information see Section Four, Skill 1).*

U006
E3

If you are a good listener other members of your team may often come to you for advice or support. Most people think of counsellors as being professionals (like marriage guidance counsellors) but many of us reassure and support others using similar skills. You may find that:

- you need to support other members of your team.

- people often come to you for advice.

- you are a supervisor and need to counsel your staff.

If so, use the following self-check to assess your own advising and supporting skills.

SELF-CHECK ## Advising and supporting skills

Do you...	Yes	No
• notice when someone's behaviour changes, e.g. they become moody and they don't seem to be working well?	☐	☐
• ask them directly what is wrong and if you can help?	☐	☐
• make sure people can trust you and know that you won't gossip about them?	☐	☐
• encourage the other person to talk by:		
– asking open questions *(see Section Two, Skill 2)* to find out what they are worried about?	☐	☐
– listening carefully? *(see Section Three, Skill 1)*	☐	☐
• offer reassurance by:		
– showing interest and concern?	☐	☐
– letting people know that they are not alone in having these kinds of problems?	☐	☐
• help people to think their problems through by:		
– asking questions which will get the other person to work through their own answer to the problem, e.g. 'What would you like to do about . . .?'	☐	☐
– suggesting some tentative ideas in the form of questions, e.g. 'How about . . .? Have you tried . . .?'	☐	☐
• help by finding out where information and/or professional help can be obtained?	☐	☐
• provide information but try not to give opinions or criticise?	☐	☐
• encourage the other person to return if they need to?	☐	☐

U010
E2

1.1b **Telephone at least two organisations on your contact list and find out what help they can provide.**

Write a few lines about the kind of help available from each organisation.

GIVING AND RECEIVING CRITICISM

Everyone has a right to know how they are doing and what they can do to improve. That's what criticism is all about. However, most of us aren't very good at receiving criticism; if someone says something nice about us we tend to get embarrassed and if they say something bad, we get angry or upset! We should really try to handle criticism ourselves before we begin to criticise others!

Criticism is only worthwhile if you can accept it and act upon it. Try not to take it personally. The following tips might help.

Receiving criticism

Do	Why?
Listen carefully.	This is so that you avoid jumping to the wrong conclusions and make sure that you respond only to the facts.
Be fair.	The criticism may be deserved.
Express your own feelings and opinions.	Perhaps you have a genuine problem and could discuss it?
Use the criticism positively and ask open questions to find out more e.g. 'How can I improve before I apply again?'	You may be able to get advice which will help you next time.
Say 'Sorry', if it's appropriate, but be positive, e.g. 'Sorry, but I know I can do better next time.'	This will stop your confidence from being dented.
Try to remain calm, even when the criticism isn't deserved.	You will earn more respect.
Ignore any rude or abusive criticism.	This sort of criticism is unlikely to be justified.

1.2a Think of some examples of people that you would like to criticise at work.

> Write down exactly what it is that makes you upset or angry.

Your list may have included things like:

- he's always late.

- she is always off on Mondays!

- their standard of work isn't very good. Two customers have complained about poor service this week.

- he has touched me three times already today!

- she's always interrupting me when I'm trying to do something.

- she notices my mistakes but never says when I do something well.

If you have been very specific, like the examples above, you have got a good starting point for giving criticism. Use the following self-check to prepare for when you need to give criticism:

SELF-CHECK Giving criticism

Do you...	Yes	No
• avoid being personal and stick to the facts and figures? (e.g. 'Quality Control have noticed a 20 per cent increase in rejects from your area'.)	☐	☐
• make sure that you're honest and don't avoid the truth?	☐	☐
• give the other person an opportunity to explain how they feel?	☐	☐
• make some suggestions on how the other person could improve?	☐	☐
• agree a course of action with the other person?	☐	☐
• make sure that you give criticism in private?	☐	☐

| MOTIVATING PEOPLE

Getting the best from any team is an important skill. Motivation is the 'drive' or inner force that helps us achieve our goals. At work, motivation is the key to getting results. Whether you are a team member or a team leader, it will help if you can use different ways to motivate yourself or your workmates.

1.3a Think about the kind of things that encourage you to work harder. Ask your friends about the kind of things which encourage them to do a good job.

Make a list of these things.

There has been lots of research into motivation and this has found that people are motivated by different needs:

- we all need things to live like food, water, air and sleep. You may be motivated by rewards like a bar of chocolate when you have finished a task! Generally, people will work less well if they are overtired, hungry or work in a stuffy atmosphere.

- we all have a need for safety and to be free from harm. People feel happier at work if they work in a healthy and safe environment.

- people like to belong to a group. This is partly why more employers are encouraging staff to work in teams.

- everyone likes to be respected by others and so can be motivated by genuine praise.

- people want to be able to do their job well and to be able to achieve their own potential.

Your list will depend on whom you asked but other people have said they are motivated by:

- doing a job which interests them.

- getting paid!

- being praised and rewarded.
- being respected at work.
- being consulted.
- getting results and being able to see that they have achieved something.
- feeling safe – often because there is good communication and they know what is happening.

1.3b **Make a list of some of the tasks that you have to do at work.**

1. Write down whether your motivation is high and you find it easy to get down to them, or whether your motivation is fair or poor.

2. Ask a workmate how he or she feels about the same tasks.

3. Discuss why you feel differently about them (if you do.) If you both have low motivation about the same task, think about anything that you could change to increase your motivation.

U010
E2

You could follow up this activity by suggesting any ideas you have for increasing motivation to your supervisor or team leader. See the next Skill for help with putting across your point of view. If you do this remember to tape the discussion so that you can show what you have achieved.

SKILL 4: | PUTTING ACROSS YOUR POINT OF VIEW |

There will be times when you have a brilliant idea and want to win over other members of your team. This is not always easy!

1.4a **When was the last time that you tried to persuade someone about a work-related issue? Did you succeed?**

Try to work out why you were successful or unsuccessful.

You could have tried to get someone to do something; talked a workmate into swapping shifts; or objected to or supported a change in working conditions. Selling is another example of persuasion.

You probably found you were successful when:

- you were friendly and reasonable.
- you had lots of good reasons and could support your case.
- you expressed yourself simply and clearly.
- people listened to you!
- other people supported you.

If you need to persuade others, use the following self-check to help.

Putting across your point of view

Getting ready: Have you...	Yes	No
• collected all the information you need including facts and figures?	☐	☐
• worked out what you are going to say and jotted down your main points on paper?	☐	☐
• practised saying what you want beforehand?	☐	☐
• prepared for questions and thought about your answers?	☐	☐
Speaking up: Did you...		
• make a positive statement to start with to catch people's attention?	☐	☐
• outline the benefits, giving practical examples where possible?	☐	☐
• use language that everyone could understand?	☐	☐
• finish on a strong point, stressing your point of view, and/or with what you wanted people to do?	☐	☐

Afterwards: Did you:	Yes	No
• get friends to give you their comments?	☐	☐
• think about what you would do differently next time?	☐	☐

Sometimes you may need to negotiate. This skill is covered in the next Section. If you do have to persuade people at work about something, you might want to look at it now.

SKILL 5: **BRIEFING A TEAM**

Briefings are a real opportunity to let staff know and understand what is going on and why. They are becoming much more common at work as managers and employers are realising the value of employee involvement. You should always be given the opportunity to ask questions.

A briefing normally lasts for about 10 minutes and never longer than 30 minutes. It should be a regular event – possibly first thing every morning but whenever is convenient for the team. It will usually take place wherever you work.

1.5a **Why do you think regular briefings are important at work?**

Jot down as many reasons as you can.

People have said that briefings are important because:

- they give everyone the opportunity to understand what's happening.

- people are more likely to be co-operative if they know why something is happening and are told well in advance.

- talking about work will make people more interested.

- they reduce the likelihood of gossip or rumour!

Briefings should only happen if staff need to be told something, rather than because it is briefing day! In some workplaces, a briefing every day will allow supervisors to discuss the previous day's achievements and to agree new targets. In other organisations, briefings may only need to happen when something changes.

1.5b **Do you have briefings in your workplace?**

If 'yes', when do they take place, who gives them and what are they about? Do you think they are worthwhile?

If 'no', can you think of any times when you have been 'kept in the dark' and wish that you had known what was going on? Do you think your team should be given regular briefings?

Jot down some rough notes in answer to the questions.

Briefings need to give information. They can be used to tell staff about:

- changes in working hours such as bank holiday arrangements.

- the company's results and achievements.

- new members of staff.

- changes in management.

- any training initiatives.

- any new government legislation affecting work.

You can probably add some more. Here is an example of some notes prepared for a briefing:

BRIGHT BROTHERS PLC:	**Briefing Notes**
Section: Catering	*Briefer's name:* T. Kitchen
Date: November 21	*Absentees:* Maisie & Tom
Briefing item	*Main points*
1. Current work	10% increase in staff using the canteen last month. Received lots of requests to repeat the Chinese lunchtime special. Well done.
2. Government legislation: Food Safety Act (1990)	Repeating the one day food hygiene courses for all food handlers. Next course will be in January.
3. Holidays	Must be booked at least one month in advance. (Need notice to organise cover).
4. Internal Vacancy: Dining Room Supervisor	A job specification for this post is on the noticeboard. Encourage staff to apply. Training will be provided.
5. Staff Christmas Party	Any suggestions?
6. Any questions?	

If you are responsible for briefing staff, use the following self-check to see how effective you are:

SELF-CHECK **Briefing skills**

Before briefing, do you ...	**Yes**	**No**
• prepare your brief carefully and write some notes?	☐	☐
• prepare answers for any questions you may be asked?	☐	☐
• check your brief with your supervisor or line manager?	☐	☐

When giving the brief, do you . . .	Yes	No
● say there will be a chance to ask questions at the end?	☐	☐
● say if you can't answer a question but find out and answer the questioner later?	☐	☐
● check that your team understand the brief?	☐	☐
● keep to the time allocated?	☐	☐
Afterwards, do you . . .		
● keep a copy of your brief?	☐	☐
● follow up any suggestions and comments made by your team?	☐	☐
● ask for feedback on the briefing?	☐	☐

1.5c Write down your views on team briefings. Use the notes that you prepared for brief tasks 1.5a and b. Produce several paragraphs.

U009
E2

WORK-RELATED ACTIVITIES

1A. Ask someone you know to act out the role of a workmate who needs support or reassurance. You could use the information you prepared for brief tasks 1.1a and b.

Prepare for the discussion with your workmate by using the self-check on encouraging and supporting skills. Set up a cassette recorder to tape the discussion.

Find out your workmate's worries by asking open questions. Make sure that you demonstrate your listening skills. Reassure him or her. Provide support by suggesting where your workmate can get more information and/or professional help.

Afterwards listen to the tape with your workmate. Use the self-check to see how you did.

U010
E4

1B. If you carry out briefings at work, record the meeting and keep copies of all the paperwork.

U009	U011
E1	E2

TAKING PART IN MEETINGS

In addition to team working, more and more companies are trying to improve communications and employee involvement in a drive to increase quality. This means that you are much more likely to have to attend meetings at work. Some of the meetings you may have to take part in are:

- team briefings

- working parties

- union meetings

- **quality circles** or **improvement teams** *(see Glossary)*

- one-to-one meetings with more senior staff, such as a staff development or appraisal interview or even a disciplinary interview.

This Section will help you to:

- understand and prepare for meetings

- be better at asking questions

- improve your negotiation skills

- be better at taking notes and minutes

- develop the skill of chairing meetings.

SKILL 1: | PREPARING FOR MEETINGS

Everyone gets involved in many different sorts of meetings at work. They can range from a casual chat in the canteen to an organised meeting in your department. You might have a one-to-one meeting with your supervisor, or call a meeting if you are a staff representative. Your role at each meeting might be different.

Did you know . . .

that some people estimate that they spend at least two-thirds of their time in meetings!

2.1a Think about the meetings that you attend at work. Jot down your role at each one.

Some people attend meetings:

- as an observer – to find out more.
- as a member of a team – a union meeting or a team briefing.
- to represent others – as a shop steward.
- to run the meeting – as the chairperson.

Many informal meetings don't need any rules, but some meetings at work are more formal, for example Council meetings, committees and union meetings. It helps if you understand the rules and jargon before you attend a meeting.

The agenda: is a list of things that will happen or will be discussed at the meeting. It is normally copied and circulated before the meeting so that people know what is going to be discussed and why they are there. An agenda could look like the example on page 29.

Apologies: are explanations sent in advance when someone is unable to attend a meeting.

Minutes: are notes taken during the meeting which briefly record the discussion and the decisions reached. Look at the minutes on page 28 if you want to see an example.

Chairperson: is the person who is in charge of the meeting.

Motion: is the name given to a formal proposal discussed during a meeting. Any proposal will normally have a 'mover' and a 'seconder' before a vote can take place. If you don't want to vote either for or against the motion, you 'abstain'.

Here are examples of minutes from a meeting, and an agenda (opposite):

BRIGHT BROTHERS PLC:

Improvement Group (Customer Service)

Minutes of the meeting held in the Board Room on Wednesday 11 November, 9.30-10.30 a.m.

Present: A. Brown (Chair), N. Walker (Sales Team), T. Elliot (Warehouse), M. Jones (Packing), D. Carter (Driver).

1. *Apologies:* these were received from T. Kitchen (unable to get cover due to flu epidemic).

2. *Minutes of the last meeting:* these were signed as a true record.

3. *Speed of service:* it was agreed that N. Walker should carry out a survey to find out how customers rate our speed of service. There has been a 20 per cent increase in the number of complaints over the past six months.

4. *Deliveries:* D. Carter drew attention to the reduced delivery times resulting from the investment in larger vans. Details of the cost savings will be available at the next meeting.

5. *Date of the next meeting:* The next meeting will take place on Thursday 10 December 9.30-10.30 a.m.

Signed: .... Chairperson, 10 December 1991

Formal meetings often have rules, normally because there is limited time or a lot of business to deal with. You may only be allowed to speak 'through the chair', which means you have to get permission to speak. There may be 'points of order', which are rules of the meeting. By listening carefully and observing others in the meeting you will gradually pick up the rules. You can always ask the chairperson to explain the procedures.

BRIGHT BROTHERS PLC:

Improvement Group (Customer Service)

The next meeting of the group will take place on Thursday 10 December 1991 in the Board Room, 9.30-10.30 a.m.

AGENDA

1. Apologies for absence

2. Minutes from the last meeting

3. Matters arising from the minutes

4. Results from Customer Survey – N. Walker

5. Discussion: Increasing speed of service

6. Delivery cost savings

7. Any other business

8. Date of next meeting

Quality Circle meetings are slightly different.

2.1b Read the following text:

U006
E1

'Firms face ever-stiffer competition, particularly from foreign companies setting up in Britain. The consequences are just beginning to transform production lines. In some companies cars no longer move down conveyor belts, instead they are assembled on the spot by one team of workers. In others, as in Japanese plants, workers are being encouraged to take part in a quality circle or improvement group. These usually consist of teams of 6-12 volunteers from the same work area and meet regularly to identify, analyse and solve work-related problems.'

Now describe quality circles to a friend, explaining what their function is. You could tape-record your answer instead.

Here are some questions to ask yourself next time you attend a meeting. Use the checklist to think about how well you did.

SELF-CHECK Taking part in meetings

Before the meeting: Did you...	Yes	No
• know what this meeting was about?	☐	☐
• know why you were attending it?	☐	☐
• know what was expected of you?	☐	☐
• read all the paperwork?	☐	☐
• discuss the agenda items with workmates?	☐	☐

During the meeting: Did you...		
• listen carefully?	☐	☐
• notice how others were feeling by looking out for signs of boredom, shyness or anger?	☐	☐
• ask questions when you didn't understand or wanted more information?	☐	☐
• put across your own point of view clearly?	☐	☐

After the meeting: Did you...		
• think about why the meeting was successful or unsuccessful?	☐	☐
• tell workmates what happened at the meeting?	☐	☐
• think about what you would do differently next time?	☐	☐

SKILL 2:

ASKING QUESTIONS

Asking questions is an important skill, not just in meetings but in everyday conversations.

Did you know...

that asking questions accounts for at least 25 per cent of most conversations?

Most people don't like asking questions.

25

2.2a Why are people reluctant to ask questions? Ask your friends, family or workmates and write down the reasons.

People often say they:

- feel silly.
- don't like the person they should ask.
- are too busy.
- feel they should know already.
- worry that other people will think they are dim.

Don't be afraid to ask questions. There are likely to be other people who want to know the same thing but don't dare ask for fear of being thought stupid. They will probably thank you afterwards!

Questions help you to:

- ask someone what they mean when they haven't explained it very well ('Do you mean . . .?')
- get more information ('How . . .? What . . .? When . . .? Where . . .? Who . . .? Why . . .?')
- exchange ideas ('What do you think about . . .?')
- get advice ('How could I have . . .?')
- see if someone agrees with you ('Do you agree . . .?')

10

2.2b There are different kinds of questions. Try answering these.

1. Do you have to ask questions in your work?
2. What sort of things do you have to ask most questions about in your work?
3. I'm sure you've often backed out of asking a question and later regretted it, haven't you?

You will notice that it was possible to answer question 1 by saying 'yes' or 'no'. This is called a 'closed question'. Closed questions are useful for getting specific facts and yes/no answers.

Question 2 made you give more information. This is called an 'open question'. Open questions are useful when you want more detail, or if you want to get silent or shy people to talk more.

You probably wanted to answer 'yes' to question 3. It's called a 'leading question' because the question suggests the answer the questioner wants. Watch out for these!

SKILL 3:

NEGOTIATING SKILLS

Everyone negotiates with other people. We negotiate as children over the amount of pocket money we get; as teenagers over how late we can stay out; at work over whose turn it is to make the coffee!

Negotiating can be difficult because it involves reaching an agreement from two different starting positions. Skilled negotiators like trade union representatives normally have quite a lot of training to help them. You may need to negotiate in a meeting. If you do need to negotiate at work, here are some tips to help you. You may also want to look back to Section One, Skill 4 to remind yourself of the skills needed for putting across your point of view.

Negotiating skills

Do	Don't
Prepare your case beforehand. What do you want to achieve? Have you got the support of your workmates?	Enter into any discussions without preparation.
Think about the arguments which may be used against you and prepare answers.	Ignore other people's arguments and just re-state your own.

Do	Don't
Concentrate on general interests e.g. to get more money, to have a more stimulating job. Be prepared to give and take.	Take up a position, e.g. 'I must have promotion within six months'. (This could be the end of any discussions!)
Think about the advantages and disadvantages of any suggestions made by the other person.	Dismiss ideas straight away. (This could lead to a disagreement)
Keep the discussion to the problem.	Criticise or attack the other person.
Stick to the facts.	Exaggerate. Comments like 'That is completely unreasonable', will irritate the other person.
Disagree constructively: give reasons first and then say 'and that is why I disagree'.	Disagree first – the other person may not listen to your reasons.
Be open about your thoughts and feelings. The other person will tend to think that you are honest and helpful.	'Keep your cards close to your chest'. The other person will be trying to guess what you are up to and is likely to be suspicious.
Ask questions. You will get more information and can also use them as a means of putting forward suggestions.	Assume that you understand the other person's point of view.
Make sure that you get any agreement in writing.	Rely on verbal agreements when the issue is important.

2.3a Think about something that you've wanted for ages. At work this could be protective clothing, or a shorter lunch break so that you can finish earlier and collect your children from school. Make some notes to support your case and jot down some ideas about how the other person may respond.

Use the tips to practise your negotiating skills at home and at work.

SKILL 4: | TAKING NOTES AND MINUTES |

Being able to take notes is an important skill for anyone at work. Notes will help you to get things down in a structured way when you have to:

- prepare a report or minutes of a meeting.

- remember what was agreed between you and a supervisor or manager.

- remember what you want to say (or what was said) during a telephone call.

Note-taking tips

- keep them short.

- use headings and key points.

- include dates, times, places, people involved.

- use abbreviations.

- number the pages.

- try drawings, lists, tables, anything that will jog your memory.

- highlight the key words and points using underlining, coloured pens or boxes.

- remember you don't have to write sentences or put words down in any particular order if the notes are for your own use.

- allow plenty of space, as you may want to add things later.

- you don't need to take notes in straight lines. Lots of people prefer to take pattern notes, which look like the example on page 35.

2.4a This task will help you practise your note-taking skills. Listen to a news broadcast on the radio. Make notes of the important points as they are made. If you can, record the broadcast then play it back to see how well you have summarised the important facts.

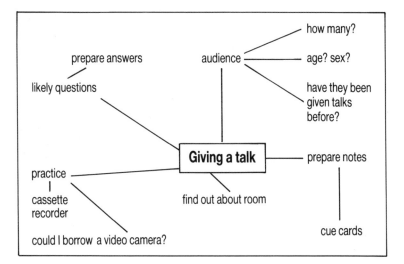

Taking notes from official meetings is called 'minuting'. These minutes are very important because they are a written record of the meeting and should prevent misunderstandings of what was said or what action was proposed. Most people worry when they are asked to take minutes, in case they get it wrong, but you can always check afterwards with the people who were there so don't panic!

There may be times when you do need to write down something word-for-word. For example, you could be taking a statement from a witness to an accident or you may need an accurate record of an agreement. Ask people to repeat slowly what they have said and if they still go too quickly for you to write it down, interrupt them and ask if they could wait until you have finished. When you write minutes, use the self-check:

SELF-CHECK **Writing minutes**

Before writing did you ...	Yes	No
• take good clear notes of the meeting?	☐	☐
• keep a copy of the agenda so that you can use the same headings and numbers?	☐	☐
• make sure you can write them up while the details are fresh in your mind?	☐	☐

Have you...	Yes	No
● included the time, place, the people who came and those who sent apologies?	☐	☐
● summarised the main points and discussions?	☐	☐
● noted the main decisions and any action that has to be taken?	☐	☐
● included people's names where you think it is important?	☐	☐
● recorded any proposals or motions and how many voted for, and how many against, any decisions?	☐	☐
● included the date of the next meeting?	☐	☐

U009
E1

2.4b Take your own notes at the next meeting you attend. Practise writing them up as minutes. The time for this activity will depend upon the length of the meeting!

The best way to learn minuting is to practise. Why not ask if you can take the minutes at a meeting?

SKILL 5: | CHAIRING MEETINGS

Formal meetings are usually controlled by a chairperson but you may also be asked to organise and run informal meetings as part of your job. Many people don't like meetings because they think they are a waste of time and they could be doing 'proper' work. They get fed up with meetings that ramble on and run late and when they don't understand what is going on. It helps if everyone knows what the meeting is about.

Did you know ...

it is estimated that most managers talk for at least 80 per cent of the time at meetings and then thank everyone for their contributions!

2.5a Think of a meeting that you have attended recently. Jot down the reasons for having it.

There are only a few reasons for having meetings. You might have said:

- to give or exchange information as in a briefing session.

- to solve a problem, e.g. you need to improve sales.

- to make a decision.

- to express feelings or opinions, e.g. some staff are unhappy about new bonus arrangements.

- to negotiate, as in a meeting between unions and management.

If you have to run meetings as part of your job the following tips may help:

- keep the meeting short – no longer than two hours.

- make sure that the meeting won't be interrupted.

- send out an agenda giving the date, place and time of the meeting.

- start on time.

- make sure that everyone has the chance to say something.

- summarise any conclusions and actions at the end so everyone knows who is supposed to do what as a result of the meeting.

WORK-RELATED ACTIVITIES

2A. Try to persuade someone about something that you feel strongly about (you could use the notes that you prepared for brief task 2.3a). Ask a friend or colleague to play the part of the person you want to persuade.

Remember to record your discussions. You could use the self-check on putting across your point of view (see page 21) to see how well you did. Do you need to provide more information?

U010
E1

2B. If you regularly attend or run meetings at work, record the meetings and keep copies of all the paperwork. If you write an agenda, notes or minutes you could use them as part of the evidence for

U009
E1

If you are the chairperson or say something during the meeting, you could also tape the meeting as part of your evidence to show that you have achieved

U011
E2

DEALING WITH CUSTOMERS

Increased competition is forcing employers to think about their customers. Satisfied customers mean more business. Many employers are introducing or developing customer service programmes. They could be called 'customer care' or 'putting people first' and you could be asked to take part in a training course for one of these programmes.

As an employee you may be the only person that a customer comes into contact with – the 'public face' of your organisation. Any contact between you and a customer must be positive, whether you are:

- a voice at the end of a telephone

- dealing with general enquiries or complaints

- coping with lots of frustrated customers.

This Section will help you to:

- improve your listening skills so that you can find out what the customer really wants

- be better at face-to-face contact with customers

- be better at dealing with customers on the telephone

- handle complaints

- deal with conflict.

SKILL 1: | IMPROVING YOUR LISTENING SKILLS

The first stage in any customer service programme is to find out what customers need and how satisfied they are with the way you do your present job.

3.1a **Jot down answers to the following questions.**

> 1. Who are your customers?
>
> 2. What do they want from your organisation?
>
> 3. What difficulties do you face when you try to give good service?

In answer to question 1 you may have said that your customers are:

- the general public.

- 'internal customers' – other people at your place of work, for example, staff from other sections or departments.

For question 2 you could have said that they normally want you to do your job properly so that they never need to complain. Sometimes, this isn't possible.

The answers you gave for question 3 probably fall into three categories:

- things for your managers to change: for example, they could invest in better machinery, so there are fewer delays.

- things that you can change, such as giving people more information when they ask questions.

- things that no-one can do anything about, such as bad weather or accidents.

The key to good customer service is to find out what customers think about your organisation. Your managers may set up customer surveys to find out if customers are satisfied or dissatisfied with the service they receive. You might want to set up your own mini-survey – if you do this at work you may need to get permission! If you are not dealing with customers every day, you could ask five friends or neighbours for their feelings about customer care in a local store.

3.1b Use the following questionnaire to find out if your customers are happy with the service they receive.

CUSTOMER SERVICE QUESTIONNAIRE

Ask at least five customers to rate staff qualities on a scale of 1 (very poor), 2 (poor), 3 (adequate), 4 (good), 5 (excellent). Add up the scores.

Staff qualities:

Customers	Helpfulness	Efficiency	Knowledge about goods or services	Initiative	Friendliness	Total score for customer service
1.						
2.						
3.						
4.						
5.						

You can also find out what customers think by listening carefully to what they say. This sounds like common sense but most of us are really bad at listening. Test yourself:

SELF-CHECK Listening skills

Do you...	Yes	No
• sit/stand still when a customer is talking to you?	☐	☐
• look interested and look at the customer?	☐	☐
• concentrate on what is being said and avoid distractions?	☐	☐
• make listening noises (e.g. 'um', 'yes') and nod your head?	☐	☐
• ask open questions to find out more? (see Section Two, Skill 2)	☐	☐
• keep cool so that you can think carefully?	☐	☐
• make sure that you don't interrupt?	☐	☐
• summarise what the customer has said when they have finished speaking?	☐	☐

If you answered mostly 'yes', then well done! Most of us are very bad listeners because:

- we're too used to 'easy listening' on television and radio.
- we think we know what people are going to say!
- we're easily distracted and our concentration wanders.
- some people aren't very good at saying what they mean.

If you answered mostly 'no', then try to practise good listening skills.

Remember that these skills do not just apply to customers. If you are a supervisor or manager, why not change the word 'customer' to 'employee' and find out if you listen to your staff!

SKILL 2: | FACE-TO-FACE CONTACT

Dealing with people face to face is not as easy as it sounds. We all avoid people at some point because of the way they look or what they say. Our customers will only ask for help if they think we are approachable.

3.2a **Make a list of the things you would look for from a person working in a shop if you wanted to ask them for some advice.**

You would probably look for someone who:

- was friendly.
- smiled.
- was clean and smart.
- greeted you by saying 'hello' or 'can I help?' as if they really meant it.
- offered to help or was already helping someone else.

It isn't really very difficult to please people either! Most of us believe it's the little things that count. Lots of research has been done on helpful behaviour. Why not test whether you practise it?

QUESTIONNAIRE: HOW HELPFUL ARE YOU?

When dealing with people do you . . .	Tick the one which applies to you.		
	Rarely	Sometimes	Always
• Smile?			
• Make some eye contact and look at the other person?			
• Sit beside the other person, or half turned towards them?			
• Find out and use the other person's name early on in the conversation?			
• When listening, nod and make 'I'm listening' noises?			
• Ask the other person open questions?			
• Show empathy by saying you understand how the other person feels and can see things from their point of view?			
• Say when you agree with the other person and explain why?			

	Rarely	Sometimes	Always
• Make sure that you give a reason first before you say that you disagree with someone?			
• Admit when you don't know the answer or have made a mistake?			
• Clearly explain what you are doing, or hope to do, for the other person?			
• End the conversation on a positive note?			

Score: award yourself one point for each 'rarely', two for 'sometimes' and three for 'always'. If you scored:

12-18 Poor – try to improve your face-to-face communication skills.

19-29 Fair – try to build on this good foundation by developing more helpful behaviour.

30-36 Excellent – use any of the skills which were new to you to become even more helpful!

SKILL 3: | TELEPHONE SKILLS

The telephone is being used more and more as a way of communicating. It's cheaper than face-to-face meetings, more convenient and saves time. Sometimes the only contact the customer has with your place of work is the telephone and their first impression is very important. As far as that caller is concerned your voice is the company or organisation.

3.3a Make a list of all the things that annoy you when you telephone an organisation. Ask someone else if they can add anything to your list.

You probably get annoyed when:

- no-one answers the telephone.

- you're not greeted and you don't know if you've got the right number.

- no-one tells you that you're being transferred and the telephone goes dead.

- the other person just answers 'yes' or 'no' and doesn't give enough information.

- the other person doesn't listen properly.

- the other person talks too much.

You probably thought of other things too! It makes you realise that using the telephone isn't as easy as you think. When you deal with someone face-to-face you can get lots of information from their body language, facial expressions and gestures as well as hearing what they say and how they say it. On the telephone you might jump to the wrong conclusion!

When you answer the telephone at work, there are some specific standards to aim for:

SELF-CHECK Answering the telephone at work

Do you...	Yes	No
• answer the telephone promptly – within three rings if possible?	☐	☐
• smile as you pick up the receiver? This makes your voice sound friendlier!	☐	☐
• speak slowly and clearly?	☐	☐

	Yes	No
• start the call by identifying your organisation or department and your own name to the caller, e.g. 'Catering Department. Mary Brown speaking. Can I help you?'	☐	☐
• ask open questions to find out what the caller wants?	☐	☐
• listen and resist the temptation to interrupt?	☐	☐
• make notes and read back the key points so that you have a record of the call and the caller knows that you're listening?	☐	☐
• try to be helpful and volunteer information?	☐	☐
• warn callers first if you need to put the telephone down or transfer them to someone else?	☐	☐
• arrange to find out when you don't have the information and then call back so the caller doesn't have to wait?	☐	☐
• finish the conversation by going over exactly what you are going to do as a result of the conversation?	☐	☐
• give your name in case the caller needs to speak to you again?	☐	☐

If you answered mostly 'yes' then customers are likely to be happy with your response. If you answered mostly 'no', then you may find people getting annoyed.

You might be someone who needs to make telephone calls rather than receive them.

3.3b **Make up a list of golden rules for someone who needs to make telephone calls related to work.**

Did you include some of the following points?

• plan the call first.

- smile and introduce yourself (and your company if you are at work).

- say why you are ringing.

- agree any action.

- finish the call politely.

One of the most important parts of any telephone call is taking messages. Most organisations have a form for passing on telephone messages. Look at this example:

BRIGHT BROTHERS PLC   **Telephone message**

Time:... Date: ....

Message for: ....

Caller: ....

Address: ....

....

....

Tel. No:...Extension: ....

Message: ....

....

....

....

....

Message taken by: ....

3.3c Here are three different telephone conversations. Read them, and using the form as a guide, practise writing suitable messages. You can make up any additional information if needed.

1. 'Good morning. It's Anna from White's Warehousing here. Would you tell Geoff that I've got a query about his last order. Could he call me back sometime today please? My number is 061-245 572 ext. 305. Thank you.'

2. 'Good afternoon. This is the Head Teacher from St. Mary's Infant School speaking. I'm afraid that Kim Hari has fallen in the playground and has been taken to Brownhampton Hospital. Would you tell her mother that it's not serious but they are going to keep her in for observation. Could she call me or the hospital as soon as possible?'

3. 'Hello. Maisie from Catering here. We don't know how many teas you want for this afternoon's meeting. Could Leslie call us back – it's ext. 34?'

Use the following self-check to make sure that you have included all the important points.

SELF-CHECK Taking telephone messages

Have you included ...	Yes	No
• who the message is for – the person's name?	☐	☐
• the date and time of the telephone call?	☐	☐
• the caller's name? (ask them to spell it out for you, if you're not sure)	☐	☐
• his/her company and telephone number?	☐	☐
• a brief summary of the message?	☐	☐
• any action needed, e.g. will the caller call back or should the person for whom the message is for call them?	☐	☐
• your name?	☐	☐

Telephone answer machines are becoming more popular at work. Many people aren't very confident about using them. You could practise by leaving messages using a tape recorder. Rehearse the message in your mind a few times or write it down. Remember you need to give:

- your name and telephone number.

- the date and time.

- the message – lots of people leave one but you could ask to be called back instead!

SKILL 4:

HANDLING COMPLAINTS

People are generally quick to complain and slow to praise! This can be annoying when you work hard and do your job well. But it is worth thinking about complaints as valuable information on what people think of your service, not as nuisances to put up with.

3.4a Think of yourself as a customer. What are your most common complaints about shops or services? Make a list, e.g. long queues, rude staff, goods out of stock.

Here is a self-check for handling complaints:

SELF-CHECK **Handling complaints**

Do you...	Yes	No
• make sure that the customer is not kept waiting?	☐	☐
• listen carefully without interrupting?	☐	☐
• treat the customer with sympathy?	☐	☐
• follow your organisation's policy for handling complaints by either:		
– solving the problem by replacing the goods or giving a refund?	☐	☐

	Yes	No
or		
– explaining carefully to the customer why you are unable to help and calling a more senior member of staff?	☐	☐
• keep the customer informed at all times?	☐	☐
• apologise where your organisation is at fault?	☐	☐
• make sure the customer is happy and satisfied with your service?	☐	☐

If you answered mostly 'yes', your customers will probably return. If you answered mostly 'no', your customers may take their custom elsewhere!

If complaints are handled badly, customers can become aggressive or abusive. Make sure you don't do any of the following:

Don't	Example
Don't argue	'It's your mistake, not ours...'
Don't offer excuses	'I had a hangover...'
Don't blame others	'It's my boss's fault...'
Don't take it personally	'I want to go home as well you know...'
Don't make the customer feel small	'No-one else has complained. What makes you different?'
Don't make false promises	'I'm sure my boss will agree to a refund.'

Some of these comments would probably make the customer even more angry and the situation could get worse!

DEALING WITH CONFLICT

Occasionally, you might come into serious conflict with a customer. It might be:

- someone swearing or being abusive.
- a violent situation.

These are difficult to deal with and there are no right or wrong ways of handling them as different situations call for different reactions. But here are some general hints to help you cope.

- ignore personal remarks and insults.
- tell the customer you will help if they give you a chance.
- listen.
- show interest and concern.
- ask questions so that you can find what the problem is.
- apologise, where you know your organisation is at fault.
- remember that people aren't angry at you personally, they don't even know you! So try to keep cool yourself.
- try to do something to help them if you can, but be honest.

People often get angry when the situation is out of their control – for example if they get caught in a traffic jam or a train is late. They may also be worried for a relative or friend – for example if they have to wait a long time in a hospital casualty department. Often there isn't much that you can do, but they would probably appreciate a friendly gesture such as a cup of tea!

Physical violence is even more difficult and with luck you will never have to deal with it. Usually the conflict has gone beyond the stage where you can reason with the person and you are in a 'no win' situation.

Often there are hints that someone is about to lose their cool and use violence. Watch for body language carefully so that you can recognise warning signs such as clenched fists, raised voices, trembling, or the smell of alcohol. If the other person does become violent:

- don't retaliate.

- seek help from someone else.

- defend yourself or a colleague/customer but remember that legally you can use no more than the minimum amount of force required by the circumstances – you must never get in first!

- remember to report the incident.

Look at this example of an incident report form.

BRIGHT BROTHERS PLC
Incident Report Form

Date of incident: ....Day of week: ....Time: ....

Details of Employee:

Name: .... Job Title: ....

Department: ....

Describe the task you were doing at the time of the incident.

....

....

....

....

....

Details of Assailant(s):

Name(s): ....

Address(es): ....

....

....

Age: ....

Male/female: ....

Other details: ....

Details of Witness(es):

Name(s): ....

Address(es): ....

....

....

Age: ....

Male/female: ....

Other details: ....

Describe the incident, including any relevant events leading up to it:

....

....

....

What was the result of the incident? Injury? Verbal abuse? Damage to property?

....

....

How much time was lost? ....

Is there likely to be legal action? ....

Where did the incident take place? ....

Any other relevant information: ....

....

3.5a Practice filling in an incident report form. Use the details of an incident that you know about or make up the information. This sentence might help you to get started: 'I was putting a parking ticket on a car windscreen when the owner returned. He started arguing . . .'

Remember satisfied customers and those whose complaints are dealt with properly are unlikely to be difficult, and are more likely to think positively about your organisation.

WORK-RELATED ACTIVITIES

3A. Use your survey results to decide on how good customer care really is in your workplace or local shop. Write down your views. You should produce several paragraphs of writing.

U009
E2

3B. If you deal with customers, either face-to-face or on the telephone, every day at work, tape-record some of your conversations. Use the self-checks to see how good your customer care skills are.

U010
E1&/or E2&/or E3

GIVING TALKS AND PRESENTATIONS

You probably think that you'll never be asked to give a talk or presentation and know that you will try to avoid it if you possibly can! But you are more likely to have to speak to a group at work now than you were a few years ago. You might be asked to:

- give the feedback for your group during a training course
- give a talk on the work of your section to new employees, visitors or a group of managers
- give a presentation if you are promoted
- talk during a workplace discussion.

Everyone feels nervous about speaking up in front of a group, especially for the first time. But it does get easier the more you practise and build up your confidence.

This Section will help you to:

- find information to help you prepare your material
- prepare your talk
- understand the importance of body language
- use visual aids
- talk to a group.

SKILL 1: | FINDING THINGS OUT

Anyone who has to give a talk (or write a report) needs to have accurate and relevant information about their topic. You may need to do some background research before you start.

4.1a Think of a work-related topic (or a hobby) which really interests you. It might be health and safety, computers or job sharing. Jot down as many sources of information as you can think of.

You might have included:

- other people at work, managers and union representatives.

- your local Citizens' Advice Bureau.

- your public library or local college library.

- national organisations like the Health and Safety Executive (HSE) or the Trades Union Congress (TUC).

You will be able to find local addresses in the telephone directory. It is always a good idea to keep a contact list of names, telephone numbers and addresses of useful people and organisations.

Remember to update it when you come across new sources of information.

4.1b Make a contact list. You could list people that you often need to telephone at work or make a general list of useful numbers. You could make a list related to your topic above.

Once you know where to obtain the information, you need to contact the organisations by telephone, letter or in person.

One of the best sources of information is your local public library. They are often open outside normal working hours and cost nothing to join. All you have to do is prove that you live or work in the area, so take along evidence of your address (a letter, driving licence, rentbook, etc.). Librarians are information experts so do ask for help and advice. If they don't have the books in stock, they will be able to order them for you and tell you where else you could try. Libraries don't just lend books. They have:

- information about most local organisations.

- very useful reference sections.

U006
E3

- quiet areas to sit and work.

- photocopying machines so that you can take information away with you.

4.1c Decide on a topic which interests you (it could be the one that you used earlier). Go to your local library and ask if they have any information, books or magazines on this topic. See if there is any other help they can give you.

SKILL 2:

PREPARING YOUR TALK

Once you have done your background research you need to think about the people you will be talking to. Ask yourself:

- what do they already know?
- why are they there?
- what do they expect?

4.2a Think about the audience at a talk or presentation that you have recently given or listened to. Jot down some important information about them (e.g. age).

You may have written about:

- the number of people.
- how old they were.
- their status.
- their attitude.

- whether they were used to listening.
- their experience and knowledge of the topic.

It is important to research the audience as well as the topic. A talk to a group of supervisors will be very different from a talk to a group of students or youth trainees.

There are other things you need to think about as well:

- **the time of day** – many people feel very sleepy after lunch. How can you wake them up?

- **concentration problems** – most people are fairly good at concentrating for the first twenty minutes but after that it gets harder. Try to keep your talk or presentation as short as possible.

- **seating arrangements** – it's probably best to ask a small group to sit in a single row arranged in a horseshoe shape.

The next stage is to structure your talk. What you say must be clear and logical. You need to make sure that your audience understands what you are saying. This is easier if you have clear divisions:

- **beginning** – your introduction.

- **middle** – your main points.

- **end** – your conclusions.

You will probably worry about remembering what you are going to say so you might want to start by:

- preparing some pattern notes *(see Section Two, Skill 4)*.

- picking out the main headings and key points.

You might want to write out your talk as a way of preparing. This makes some people feel more confident, but don't read out your entire talk word by word as this can be boring for the audience. It is much better to make up the words from your notes as you go along because people feel that you are talking to them and you come across as being more relaxed.

Your main points can be written on:

- **sheets of paper** – use a coloured pen to highlight the important points or separate out sections. Paper will rustle if you are nervous so you may find it better to use:

- **small filing (or index) cards** – you will have enough room on these for your main points and they are easy to handle. Remember to number them! These can be called cue cards.

- **overhead projector transparencies and flip charts** – (*see Skill 3 on page 60*, Using visual aids).

These main points may also be called presentation or speaking notes. Look at this example of cue cards for a talk on 'Setting up your own business':

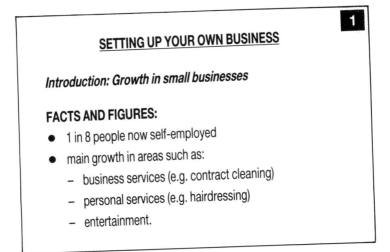

1

SETTING UP YOUR OWN BUSINESS

Introduction: Growth in small businesses

FACTS AND FIGURES:
- 1 in 8 people now self-employed
- main growth in areas such as:
    - business services (e.g. contract cleaning)
    - personal services (e.g. hairdressing)
    - entertainment.

Main Points: Help available

2a

JOBCENTRES FOR INFORMATION ABOUT:
- Enterprise awareness events
- Business advice and counselling
- Business planning
- Business training.

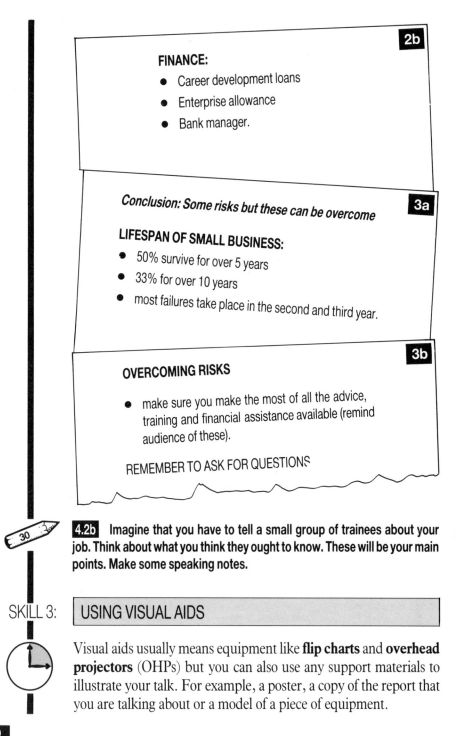

FINANCE:

- Career development loans
- Enterprise allowance
- Bank manager.

2b

Conclusion: Some risks but these can be overcome

3a

LIFESPAN OF SMALL BUSINESS:

- 50% survive for over 5 years
- 33% for over 10 years
- most failures take place in the second and third year.

3b

OVERCOMING RISKS

- make sure you make the most of all the advice, training and financial assistance available (remind audience of these).

REMEMBER TO ASK FOR QUESTIONS

4.2b Imagine that you have to tell a small group of trainees about your job. Think about what you think they ought to know. These will be your main points. Make some speaking notes.

SKILL 3: | USING VISUAL AIDS

Visual aids usually means equipment like **flip charts** and **overhead projectors** (OHPs) but you can also use any support materials to illustrate your talk. For example, a poster, a copy of the report that you are talking about or a model of a piece of equipment.

Did you know...

> *people only remember about one third of the content of a talk or presentation. Using visual aids will help your audience to remember much more.*

45

U007

E3

4.3a Collect some examples of information which is presented visually, e.g. tables, bar charts, pie charts and graphs (see Glossary). Try to include at least three tables such as timetables, conversion charts, price lists or planner charts. Do you think that they are good ways of presenting information? Make sure that you understand how they can be used.

Using visual aids can give you more confidence but they must back up whatever it is you are talking about. (They are not required for Stage 1 of the C&G Certificate). If you are giving a presentation at work you may want to use an OHP or a flip chart. They can help to:

- summarise your main points.

- present your notes.

- display information in a way which is easy to understand.

30

4.3b Prepare a visual aid to accompany your talk to the trainees. This could be a timetable of your day which you use as a handout; one or two OHP transparencies or flip chart sheets which summarise your main points. Use the self-check below as a guide.

SELF-CHECK Using visual aids

Have you...	Yes	No
• given two or three main points only?	☐	☐
• checked that everyone can see it clearly?	☐	☐
• highlighted the main points?	☐	☐
• made sure that it looks neat and tidy?	☐	☐
• checked the spelling?	☐	☐

When you use a flip chart, do you ...	Yes	No
• write the sheets up well in advance of your talk, if possible?	☐	☐
• stop talking if you have to write during your presentation?	☐	☐
If you use an OHP, do you ...		
• prepare your transparencies beforehand?	☐	☐
• put the screen to one side (your right-hand side if you are right-handed) so that people can see it?	☐	☐
• keep your face towards your audience when you use the transparencies?	☐	☐
• set up the machine before you start and practise using it?	☐	☐

SKILL 4: | **BODY LANGUAGE**

Body language is how we communicate without words. It is sometimes called non-verbal communication. It is very important when you are giving a talk or a presentation because it is part of putting yourself across and making people want to listen to you. Most body language is unconscious – everyone has their own facial expressions and physical mannerisms.

4.4a Watch a variety of television programmes. Observe some television personalities and make some notes describing their body language. Say whether you think their mannerisms help them to get their message across. (You might find it easier to concentrate on body language if you turn the sound down).

Here are some examples:

• Mrs Thatcher (forcefulness, loud voice, leans forward when she talks, speaks slowly to make a point).

- Terry Wogan (raises eyebrows, cheeky grin to create relaxed atmosphere).

- Ian McCaskill, the weatherman (uses arm gestures to reinforce his point).

Some mannerisms you could look out for are:

- banging on the table to make a point.

- leaning back in a chair. This generally reveals a relaxed person.

- feet tapping the floor or drumming a pencil on the table could indicate boredom.

- twisting rings or playing with jewellery could suggest nervousness.

- a louder than normal voice could show anger.

Body language helps you to appear natural but if you are too nervous your mannerisms can be annoying to the audience and you may not come over very well. People who are very nervous tend to twitch and scratch, click pen tops or jangle keys. They also use too many *'ums'* and *'arrs'* as they talk. You could ask a friend to tell you about your own body language!

When you are speaking to a group, think about the messages your body language is giving to your audience. Try to:

- look at the people you are talking to. If your head is buried in your notes or you are staring into space, people will tend to drift off.

- smile.

- breathe deeply before you start and between your main points, to calm your nerves.

- use gestures to stress key points.

- use your voice to emphasise the important words.

4.4b Practise giving the talk on your job that you prepared earlier. Use your visual aids. Use a tape recorder if possible.

Play back and assess your own performance.

Did your talk ...	Yes	No
• flow fairly freely?	☐	☐
• get over the points you wanted?	☐	☐
• avoid too many hesitations or mistakes?	☐	☐
• co-ordinate well with your visual aids?	☐	☐

Remember, don't worry if it wasn't perfect the first time. The more you practise the better it will become.

Did you know . . .

in a survey, 30,000 Americans were asked what they feared most. 41 per cent said 'Having to speak to a group of people'.

SKILL 5: | GIVING A TALK

You should now be ready to have a go at giving a formal talk or presentation. Check all the arrangements like the room and the seating in advance. Make sure that you have your notes and that all the equipment works. Use the following self-check as a reminder:

SELF-CHECK Giving a talk

Did you ...	Yes	No
• place yourself where you felt most comfortable?	☐	☐
• check that everyone could see and hear you?	☐	☐

	Yes	No
• start by saying who you were, why you were there and what you were going to talk about?	☐	☐
• look at the people you were talking to?	☐	☐
• try to be natural and use a friendly tone?	☐	☐
• use plain English and avoid jargon and technical terms?	☐	☐
• include practical examples and your own experiences?	☐	☐
• use pauses and gestures to give emphasis?	☐	☐
• keep an eye on your watch or a clock and make sure that you finish on time?	☐	☐
• have an interesting ending so people had something to remember?	☐	☐
• thank people for listening?	☐	☐

It's best to ask people to wait until after your talk to answer questions. Think ahead to what might be asked and prepare your answers. This will help you feel more confident.

WORK-RELATED ACTIVITIES

4A. Find three to six people who will be willing to listen to you give a presentation on 'My Job'. Use the notes and visual aids that you prepared for the brief tasks (4.2b and 4.3b). Make sure that you practise beforehand (4.4b). Be prepared to answer questions. Remember to tape your talk.

U011
E2

4B. If you give a briefing, talk or verbal report, keep a copy of your speaking notes and tape the talk.

U011
E2

4C. Next time you attend a briefing, talk or presentation, or watch a training video, listen carefully and make notes of the key points. Observe the presenter carefully and pick up some tips on talking to groups.

U012
E1 and/or E2

GETTING THE MOST OUT OF TRAINING

In the past, it has mainly been professional and managerial employees who have been given the chance to be trained. This is changing. The move to a **Single European Market** has increased the pressure on British companies to be competitive and it is recognised that there are shortages of skilled workers in many occupations. This means that everyone is now more likely to be asked to take part in training. You may need to:

- keep your skills up to date and adaptable if you are in work

- retrain if you want to change jobs

- learn new skills if you are out of work

- gain more skills if you want to progress

- take part in training in order to comply with government legislation such as health and safety or food hygiene.

This Section will help you to:

- take part in training
- find out about training opportunities
- get ready for training

- prepare for assessment
- take advantage of a staff development interview or appraisal.

SKILL 1:

TAKING PART IN TRAINING

Once you have decided to take part in training you need:

- confidence.
- motivation.

- an idea about your own interests and abilities.

and specific study skills:

- reading skills *(see Section Seven, Skill 1)*
- note-taking skills *(see Section Two, Skill 4)*
- asking questions *(see Section Two, Skill 2)*
- writing skills *(see Section Seven, Skills 2 and 3)*.

As you can see, each of these skills is covered in other Sections so this Section will concentrate on helping you to increase your confidence and motivation.

Lots of people are really worried about taking part in training and need to overcome their fears before they start.

Do you ever think:	If yes, then remind yourself:
I'm too old to benefit from training.	One in forty adults in the UK have studied successfully with the Open University in the last twenty years.
I'm happy in my job and want to stay as I am.	Unfortunately, job security is a thing of the past.
I'm not clever enough to take part in training.	Who says? If a man with hardly any 'O' levels can become Prime Minister . . .!
It'll be just like going back to school. I hated school!	Learning as an adult is really different but you'll only find out if you give it try!
I don't need training. It's only for people who want to get a job.	Everyone can be better at what they do.

The secret to successful learning is gaining the confidence to believe that you can do it and the motivation to want to do it! If you want to increase your confidence and see how good you are, look at page 79 and complete brief task 6.1a.

5.1a To increase your motivation, write down all the reasons why you want to take part in training. Think of as many as you can and then compare with the list below.

Other people have said that they want to take part in training:

- to learn new skills.

- to be better at their jobs.

- to keep up to date.

- to be prepared for change.

- to be more confident.

- to gain promotion or more money.

- to get a qualification.

- to get back into studying.

- to be able to impress customers, boss or colleagues.

Remember, the more reasons you have for wanting to study, the more likely you are to be successful!

Did you know ...

> *that the average adult has sixty-one hours a week of free time (not spent at work or sleeping). Why not think about putting a few hours aside for training?*

SKILL 2: | FINDING OUT ABOUT TRAINING OPPORTUNITIES |

You may have decided that you want to improve your skills and/or gain some qualifications. But what help is available and where do you go to find out more?

5.2a Think about where you could get help. Ask a friend or colleague at work if they know who to ask or where to go. Jot down some ideas.

You might have thought about:

- a careers office.
- a Jobcentre.
- your local library.
- your local college.
- the training/personnel department at work or your supervisor.

You could also try:

- **your Training and Enterprise Council (TEC)** – (called **local enterprise companies** in Scotland). They are organisations headed by employers and staffed by training experts. There are 82 TECs in England and Wales and 22 local enterprise companies in Scotland, so there will be one near you. They are responsible for ensuring that you can get advice and guidance about:

  - training for a new job.
  - adding to your existing skills.
  - setting up or expanding your own business.

- **an Education Shop or High Street Information Centre** can provide advice and information about training.

- **Training Access Points (TAPs)** are computer terminals which you can use to find out about all the training opportunities in your area. There may be a TAP in your local library or even in your supermarket!

- **your local college** will run lots of courses related to work.

- **your trade union** probably runs a wide range of education courses. Your full-time Official or Regional Education Officer can give you more information. Ask your shop steward for a telephone number.

- **Open Learning** is a good option if you have difficulty attending a course regularly. You normally work from workbooks (like this one!) or use computers and videos to obtain information and answer questions. At an open learning centre you can get support from a tutor. **Distance learning** is similar but you normally work from home. You can still get telephone support from a tutor.

5.2b If you want to find out more:

1. Ask about TECs and TAPs at your local Jobcentre.

U010
E2

2. Ask to see a copy of the Open Learning Directory at your local Jobcentre. Make a note of any courses which interest you.

U006	U010
E3	E2

3. Write to the Open College and see what courses are available.

U009
E1

4. Find out the number of your local college from the telephone book. Ring and ask for a prospectus.

U006	U010
E3	E2

Once you know where to go for information, it helps if you understand the jargon. The following terms and abbreviations are frequently used by people in training:

Competency based training:

Is the term used to describe how qualifications have been broken down into a range of elements (called competences). You need to prove your competence by showing that you can carry out tasks and activities to a pre-set standard. This means that you can work towards a qualification over any period of time and by a variety of methods. All NVQs *(see below)* are competence based.

Accreditation of Prior Learning (APL):

This is a process which gives you a qualification for what you already know and do. For example, if you have work experience, a hobby or care for children or an elderly/disabled person you can get credit for these skills. A skilled APL adviser will talk to you about your experience and help you gather evidence to prove your competence. This evidence will need to be presented for assessment.

Action Planning:

You could draw up your own action plan or ask a training adviser to help. It should tell you where you are now, your targets for learning new skills and dates for achieving them.

National Vocational Qualifications (NVQs) (SVQs in Scotland):

These are qualifications which are based on standards of competence for specific jobs. You should be able to get these qualifications at work but they are also available in colleges.

Did you know . . .

that it is possible to gain a competency based qualification in less than a day? An unqualified chef had over 20 years experience as a pastry cook. He was able to get a qualification when he took a collection of photographs of his work and a letter from his employer to an APL adviser in his local college.

Finding out about training

Do you . . .	Ask about . . .
want advice and guidance because you're not sure about what you want to do?	counselling and/or action planning.
want some help with spelling, writing or number before you start?	basic skills training.
believe that you are already well skilled although you don't have any qualifications?	getting a qualification for the skills that you already have (APL).
want to get a qualification?	qualifications in a subject which interests you.
want help with childcare?	a crèche or childcare allowance.
need help with money because you are unemployed or low paid?	training vouchers, career development loans and grants.
need to study at a time and place to suit you?	open and distance learning opportunities.

5.2c Make an appointment to discuss training opportunities with the person responsible in your workplace. Before the meeting make a list of questions that you want to ask. Use the advice above to help. If you prefer, see a local educational guidance worker or a tutor from your local college.

U010
E2

SKILL 3:

PREPARING FOR TRAINING

There are lots of different types of training courses and training methods:

One-to-one coaching is the name given to the informal training which takes place on the job. A supervisor or more experienced worker may coach you when you are new to the job or if you need to learn a new skill. Coaching may also help if you keep making mistakes or when you do your job well so that you know why you are successful or unsuccessful.

If you are coached at work use the following self-check to get the most from the experience:

SELF-CHECK Being coached at work:

Have you...	Yes	No
• been prepared properly so that you know exactly what you are going to learn?	☐	☐
• listened carefully?	☐	☐
• asked questions to check that you understood?	☐	☐
• made suggestions if appropriate and discussed your ideas with your coach?	☐	☐
• planned what you want to learn next?	☐	☐

Short training courses at work. These cover topics like Induction, Health and Safety, Customer Care, Management Skills or even Pre-

Retirement Training. Find out if your organisation offers in-house courses and see if anything interests you.

Open or distance learning. Studying by this method can be harder than attending a course because you have to get yourself organised, get down to it and stick at it! It can also be lonely if you work on your own.

If you are thinking seriously about taking part in training, use the following self-check to help yourself get prepared. It applies to both attending courses and to open learning.

SELF-CHECK Getting ready for training

Ask yourself:	You could ...
Do you know enough about the course?	Ask if someone can come and introduce it. Ask if you could see some of the materials. Talk to someone who is already studying.
Will it help you improve yourself?	Check that the materials are related to your job. Find out if it will help you in the future.
Are you worried about studying?	Find out what support is available. Can you contact your tutor by telephone? Do the students form self-help groups? Is there anyone at work who will help you?
How will you find time to study?	Make sure that you have set aside some time for study. Make sure that you are not disturbed.
How will you make useful notes during lectures or from books?	Read Section Two, Skill Four.

ASSESSMENTS

The trainer or tutor will want to find out how successful the training has been in helping you to learn new skills. Traditionally, exams have done this and these are still common.

However, with NVQs more tutors and trainers are introducing assessments which can be carried out at work or wherever the training has taken place. The assessment will require you to carry out a task to show that you have learnt the skills. You will need to show that you can carry out the task to the required standards. These standards are called **performance criteria** and you can find out what they are by asking a tutor. You need to collect evidence that you have completed the tasks. This is called a **portfolio** and has to be presented to an assessor.

This book is an example of how you collect evidence to prove that you can carry out tasks to the required standards. This self-check should also help:

SELF-CHECK Collecting evidence for a portfolio

Have you...	Yes	No
• kept copies of the paperwork, books, etc., which you used to help you carry out the tasks?	☐	☐
• kept copies of all your written work including first drafts and letters sent off requesting information?	☐	☐
• asked a responsible person to witness your work (particularly where you carry out the tasks in your workplace) and certify that you have carried out the task successfully? Ask them to send you a letter to prove this. You could ask your supervisor or training officer or anyone who has qualified as a workplace assessor.	☐	☐

	Yes	No
• kept detailed notes to show the assessor how you approached and carried out the task?	☐	☐
• kept a record of any oral work, for example, telephone conversations, discussions, meetings, interviews or talks, on tape?	☐	☐
• thought about taking photographs of any interesting work or activities?	☐	☐

Usually people prefer assessments rather than formal tests. They are often more realistic than tests which are very unfair if you have a poor memory and suffer from nerves after years away from studying.

SKILL 5:

STAFF DEVELOPMENT INTERVIEWS AND APPRAISALS

You may discuss what training you need in a staff development interview or appraisal. The interview should be an honest attempt to identify strengths and weaknesses at work. It is a good way of finding out how your performance at work is rated and how you could improve. The interview should be a two-way process and is an excellent way of working towards a promotion.

If you want to get the most from your interview it is worth thinking about what you would like to happen at the end of it. For example, you may want to find out about NVQs, go on a short course or learn some new skills on the job.

5.5a Make a list of the tasks that you carry out at work. Think about how well you perform each one. If there are any that you think you should do better, training could help.

Here is an example to get you started:

Task	Rating		What to do about it
	Good	Would like to do better	
Helping Customers	✓		
Using the till		✓	Ask for more on-the-job training
Writing notes and and messages		✓	Find out about communication skills training.

SELF-CHECK Staff development interviews and appraisals

	Yes	No
Before the meeting did you ...		
• think about what you wanted to say?	☐	☐
• prepare some questions?	☐	☐
During the meeting did you ...		
• listen carefully to what was said about your performance?	☐	☐
• ask for examples where you wanted more information?	☐	☐
• ask for ideas about how you could improve your current performance?	☐	☐
• adapt your views where good suggestions were made?	☐	☐
• stand firm when you really disagreed?	☐	☐
• reach an agreement on future action and set targets and a timescale?	☐	☐

After the meeting did you ...

- follow up any ideas or suggestions that came from the meeting? ☐ ☐

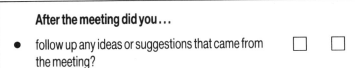

WORK-RELATED ACTIVITIES

5A. Make your own Training Development Plan. This is a record of what you want to do, what type of training you need to do it and how you plan to get the training. Use the following headings:

1. Ten things that I would like to learn. (List these, in the order of their importance to you).

2. How I am going to learn them. (e.g. ask someone to coach me on the job, open learning).

3. When I am going to learn them. (Set yourself some deadlines for finding out more and then beginning to achieve your aims).

4. Finish with a 'to do' list and get started.

| U009 |
| E1 |

5B. If you have to take part in training, or have a staff development/ appraisal interview at work, keep a record of all the paperwork. Taking notes during an interview or on a training course could be part of the evidence to show that you have achieved

| U009 |
| E1 |

Filing in a form before an appraisal could be part of the evidence to show that you have achieved

| U008 |
| E1 & E2 |

Talking to one other person during an interview could be part of the evidence to show that you have achieved

| U010 |
| E1 |

Presenting information to a group during training could be part of the evidence to show that you have achieved

| U011 |
| E2 |

APPLYING FOR A JOB OR PROMOTION

Most people can expect to have to change jobs four or five times during their working lives. If you have been in the same job since leaving school, applying for a different job, a promotion, or a new job after a redundancy can be a shock. Although some jobs are still available through word-of-mouth most employers now expect prospective employees to complete an application form and take part in a formal interview.

This Section will help you to:

- find out about job opportunities
- complete an application form and a CV
- be better at writing letters
- apply for a promotion
- do your best at an interview.

SKILL 1: FINDING OUT ABOUT JOB OPPORTUNITIES

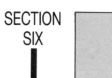

Before you start looking seriously for a job or promotion, it's best to look at yourself realistically and decide what you're good at, not so good at, and what your likes and dislikes are. This is called self-assessment and will help you decide what type of work you would like to do. It will also help you to identify your strengths and skills and work out how you can use them.

Did you know . . .

that most employers think that high levels of motivation, an interest in the job, the potential to learn new skills and the ability to get on with people are just as important as qualifications and experience?

15

6.1a Make a list of all the things that you are good at. Get a friend or colleague to make a similar list about you.

You could make a list of your weak points as well.

> For example, you may want to write 'I'm good at cooking, planning ahead, looking after children, managing money ...'

You probably found that you had more skills than you thought you did! When you go to an interview remember to emphasise your strong points and pass over your weak ones.

If you want to improve your weak points or learn some new skills, find out about training opportunities which could improve your job or promotion prospects *(see Section Five)*.

When you start to look for a job use the self-check below to find out if you are searching in the right places:

SELF-CHECK Looking for a job

Have you...	Yes	No
• checked the job vacancy cards at the Jobcentre?	☐	☐
• telephoned your local careers office to see if they offer help to adults?	☐	☐
• regularly read the advertisements in local and national newspapers?	☐	☐
• asked your family and friends to keep you informed about any jobs they know are available?	☐	☐
• contacted local employers directly by telephone or in person to ask about vacancies?	☐	☐
• looked at notices in shop windows, community centres or libraries?	☐	☐

SKILL 2:

COMPLETING AN APPLICATION FORM

Most employers will ask you to complete an application form. This form will be your first contact with an employer. It must give a good impression or the employer won't bother to interview you. Here are some form-filling hints:

- read the instructions carefully before you start.

- use a dictionary to check the meaning of any new words.

- write in pencil first, then go over it with a dark pen when you're sure it's right. You could also take a photocopy of the blank form at your local library and fill that in first for practice.

- keep your answers short and to the point.

- write n.a. (not applicable) beside any questions which do not apply to you.

- try not to cram too much information into a small space. If you need to write more use a separate piece of paper and attach it to the form.

- write something in the section at the end of the form which normally asks for any additional information. This is often the section that interviewers read most carefully. Mention your strengths and say something about why this job interests you or why you want to work for this organisation.

- keep your form neat and tidy and check all your answers carefully before you send it off.

- take a copy of your completed form. This will remind you of what you said when you go to the interview. It will also help you next time you have to fill in an application form.

Most of these form-filling hints apply to any form. If you want to be better at filling in forms collect some from work and practise on them. They could be leave requests, self-certificated sick leave, travelling expense claim forms, applications for transfer or internal promotion, requisition forms or duty sheets. You could also pick up some forms at the Post Office and practise filling them in.

6.2a Use the list of your skills and strengths. Choose five and to each one add a sentence which shows how you have demonstrated this skill. For example:

'I am good with money. I have been treasurer for our local playgroup for the last three years.'

Sometimes an employer will ask for a Curriculum Vitae (CV) rather than an application form. A CV is a summary of your education, qualifications, work experience and interests. A CV might look like this:

---

1. PERSONAL DETAILS:

Name: Maisie PARKER   *Date of Birth:* 23/8/1952

Address: 34 Redmore Gardens, Brownhampton BH2 5UT

Telephone: Brownhampton 687 654

2. EDUCATION AND TRAINING:

1986-1991 In-house courses with present employer: one day Basic Food Hygiene, two days Customer Care training, five days Introduction to Supervisory Skills.

1968-1971 Brownhampton Technical College: on a day release basis and gained City and Guilds Certificates in Catering.

1963-1968 Brownhampton Secondary School: Studied to School Certificate Level.

3. EMPLOYMENT

1986-1991 Catering Assistant, Bright Brothers PLC. Promoted to Canteen Supervisor in September 1989.

1975-1985 Housewife: various part-time jobs including cleaning, dinner-lady and shop work.

1973-1974 Head Cook, Brownhampton Cottage Hospital.

1971-1973 Cook, Brownhampton General Hospital.

1968-1971 Trainee Cook, Brownhampton General Hospital.

---

4. INTERESTS
Member of Brownhampton Players (amateur dramatics), dressmaking and walking.

5. ADDITIONAL INFORMATION:
Voluntary play group worker (1980-85).
Car owner with clean driving licence for 20 years.

6. REFERENCES:
Mr T. Kitchen, Catering Manager, Bright Brothers PLC, High Street, Brownhampton.
Dr. D. Rose, Redmore Surgery, Brownhampton.

6.2b **Write some rough notes for your own CV using the same headings as the example above.**

SKILL 3:

WRITING LETTERS

If you are applying for jobs you might have to write lots of different kinds of letters. The simplest type will probably be a letter asking for further details and/or an application form. It could look like this:

34 Redmore Gardens
Brownhampton
BH2 5UT
5/11/91

Personnel Manager
Smith's Catering Company
East Industrial Estate
Brownhampton
BH4 7TH

Dear Sir/Madam

I am writing with reference to the post of Catering Manager which was advertised in the Brownhampton Chronicle on 4/11/1991. I would be grateful if you would send me further details and an application form.

Yours faithfully

Maisie Parker

MAISIE PARKER (Mrs)

You may also need to send a full letter of application for a particular job. If Maisie had been asked to apply in writing to Mrs Jones, Personnel Manager, Smith's Catering Company, her letter could have looked like this:

34 Redmore Gardens
Brownhampton
BH2 5UT
5/11/1991

Mrs Jones
Personnel Manager
Smith's Catering Company
East Industrial Estate
Brownhampton
BH4 7TH

Dear Mrs Jones

I am writing to apply for the post of Catering Manager as advertised in the Brownhampton Chronicle on November 4.

I am currently working as Catering Supervisor in the Staff Canteen at Bright Brothers. This post involves leading a team of four assistants to produce 100 hot meals daily, run a salad bar and provide a tea and coffee service.

I am responsible for ordering stock and recording sales. I also train my staff in maintaining vending machines, using tills, food hygiene and general catering skills. I deputised for the Catering Manager last year when he spent a month in hospital.

I enjoy my present job but am keen to take on additional responsibilities and to learn some new skills. I am very interested in working for Smith's Catering Company as the company has an excellent reputation locally. I understand that there are opportunities for training and promotion.

I have enclosed my CV which gives extra information. I hope this is helpful.

I look forward to hearing from you.

Yours sincerely

Maisie Parker

MAISIE PARKER (Mrs)

6.3a Find an advertisement for a job which interests you. Write a letter in reply making sure that you set it out properly.

U006 | U009
E1 | E1

When you write any letter use the following self-check to make sure that it is good enough to send.

SELF-CHECK Writing formal letters

Have you...	Yes	No
• written the date below your address?	☐	☐
• included the name, title and address of the person you are writing to above the greeting?	☐	☐
• used the correct name or title in the greeting?	☐	☐
• stated clearly what the purpose of your letter is?	☐	☐
• used a new paragraph for new points?	☐	☐
• proofread for spelling and punctuation errors?	☐	☐
• said what you wanted to say and said it in a logical order?	☐	☐
• made sure that your writing is easy to read and that there are no crossings out?	☐	☐
• used the correct ending?	☐	☐

SKILL 4: **APPLYING FOR PROMOTION**

Applying for a promotion at work is slightly different. The person reading your application form and interviewing you will know you. They may have already formed an opinion about your suitability for the post that you are applying for. This will be based on their assessment of how well you cope with your present job and how you will be able to cope with new responsibilities. Try to do some preparation beforehand:

- ask your supervisor or boss for advice
- research the types of job which could be open to you by:
  - checking the notice boards
  - obtaining copies of any vacancy lists or staff newsletters.
- ask if you can see examples of a Job Description (this describes the tasks and responsibilities involved in the job) and a Person Specification (this should identify the skills, knowledge and experience needed to do the job).

6.4a Read the following extract from a job description and person specification:

| Job description | Person Specification | |
The main duties are:	Essential	Desirable
1. Preparing a wide range of hot meals, salads and snacks.	Previous experience Willingness to take part in food hygiene training. Understanding of stock rotation.	C&G 706/1 & 2
2. Table clearing and washing up.	Ability to follow cleaning procedures.	
3. Till duties during lunchtime service.	Ability to work under pressure. Ability to handle money and give change. Ability to get on with a wide range of people.	
4. Deal with paperwork as required (e.g. complete order forms, check deliveries, etc.)	Ability to write clearly.	

Now describe the main duties involved in this job to a friend, stating whether qualifications are essential or desirable. (You could tape your answer instead.)

You could also assess yourself as a personnel officer might. Try the next brief task:

6.4b Imagine that you are thinking of applying for promotion at work. Given your current job performance, how would you appear to an interviewer? Rate yourself by ticking the appropriate box.

Person specification	very good	satisfactory	need to improve
Appearance			
Enthusiasm for job			
Adaptability			
Ability to get on with others			
Health			
Ability to cope under pressure			
Achievements			
Willingness to learn new skills			
Interests			
Reliability			

Can you think of any other qualities your employer may be looking for?

If you have any ticks in the 'need to improve' column, think about how you could do better in the future.

SKILL 5:   ## COPING WITH INTERVIEWS

Everyone worries about interviews but they are not so bad if you do some preparation and know what to expect. The golden rule is to be yourself! Use the following self-check to prepare yourself:

SELF-CHECK **Preparing for an interview**

Have you...	Yes	No
found out as much about the organisation and the job as you can?	☐	☐
read through the job and person specifications?	☐	☐
made a check-list of questions that you could be asked and thought about your answers?	☐	☐
made a list of questions to ask (about things like training, promotion prospects, duties, etc.)?	☐	☐
telephoned or written to confirm that you will be attending the interview?	☐	☐
made a trial run to test your transport arrangements and find the right place for the interview?	☐	☐
kept a copy of your application form or CV to read before the interview and for reference?	☐	☐
made a collection of information which may be of interest to your interviewer(s), e.g. certificates, letters of recommendation, samples or photographs of work?	☐	☐
ensured that you will look smart without being over-dressed?	☐	☐

6.5a Think about the kind of questions that you might be asked in an interview. Ask a small group of friends or workmates to 'brainstorm' some ideas. (See glossary). Make a list.

You could ask someone to give you a mock interview so that you can try out your interview skills.

Here are some tips for handling the interview itself:

- listen carefully.

- make eye contact with the interviewer but don't stare constantly.

- relax by taking a few deep breaths.

- speak slowly and clearly.

- ask for more information if you don't understand the question.

- 'measure' what you say. If you say too little the interviewer will not know enough about you to be able to offer you the job. If you say too much the interviewer may well be put off!

- try to relate your past experience to the job on offer. This is a good way of handling 'What would you do if . . .' questions. You can describe how you have tackled a similar situation in the past.

WORK-RELATED ACTIVITIES

6A Using the rough notes you made in Skill 2, write your own CV. See if you can find someone to type or wordprocess it for you. You could do this yourself by dropping into one of the Open Learning Centres mentioned on page 11. If you are unemployed you could do this at your Job Club.

U009
E1

6B If you apply for a job or internal promotion keep copies of all the paperwork. This should include your rough notes on things like travel arrangements, background research and mock interviews. Make sure that you have kept a copy of your application form and/or letter and copies of the job description and person specification. This could be part of the evidence to show that you have achieved

U006	U008	U009	U010
E1	E1 & E2	E1	E1 & E2

WRITING AT WORK

This Section covers the basics of reading and writing. Both are essential at work in order to exchange ideas, information, instructions, orders and requests.

You can practise extending your vocabulary so that you find it easier to choose the right word. The skills of spelling, grammar and punctuation are also covered.

Writing a report is the most demanding of all the written work that you may have to do. But it's useful to remember that if you can write reports you can cope easily with the other paperwork you may have to deal with!

This Section will help you to:

- improve your reading skills

- practise your writing basics: vocabulary and spelling

- practise your writing basics: grammar and punctuation

- draft and edit your writing

- write a report.

SKILL 1: | IMPROVING YOUR READING SKILLS

You might wonder why reading has been included in this Section. Well, reading makes writing easier because it helps you to:

- find information quickly. You may need to gather evidence, facts and figures for your writing.

- widen your vocabulary.

- think of new ideas.

There are lots of different reading methods and you probably use them all without thinking about them. They include:

- scanning
- skimming
- careful reading
- light reading
- proofreading.

Try the following quiz to see how much you know about reading methods:

7.1a Which of the five methods of reading would you use for each of the following activities at work?

(a) reading your company's health and safety policy.

(b) reading a letter you have written to a customer.

(c) reading a newspaper during your coffee break.

(d) looking up a number in a telephone directory.

(e) reading a letter from management or from your trade union.

(f) reading the instructions for using a new piece of equipment.

Your answers may differ from those below because we sometimes mix reading methods. You could have said:

(a) and (f) careful reading:
this is really your legal duty so that you work safely.

(b) proofreading:
you probably want to check that there are no typing errors or spelling mistakes.

(c) light reading:
because you were reading for pleasure although you may have scanned the television page to see if there was anything worth watching and read your horoscope carefully!

(d) scanning:
you knew what you were looking for and you ignored everything else.

(e) skimming:

you wanted to get a general idea of what the letter is about. If it seems to be interesting you may stop and read it word for word.

If you feel that you know enough about the different sorts of reading you might want to skim the rest of this Skill and move on to Skill 2. If you want to learn more about reading methods then you could read the following information carefully.

More about different reading methods:

Scanning: helps you to look for something like a word in a dictionary. You ignore everything else and let your eyes move quickly over a page until you find the bit you want.

Skimming: is fast reading to get a general picture. You are not looking for anything in particular but simply looking to see what's there.

Careful reading: is really word by word reading and even re-reading to make sure that you understand it. This type of reading is best for official letters, legal documents, forms and instructions. It's also the best method for reading to study.

Proofreading: everyone who writes anything needs to proofread for mistakes in spelling, punctuation and grammar *(see Skill 4 in this Section)*.

Light reading: is the way most of us read most of the time. You don't need to worry about understanding every word or remembering what you've read. You are reading for pleasure.

If you have to do a lot of reading at work or are studying, you might want to improve your reading speed. Most people generally read at about 200-250 words per minute – remember this will be slower for some things and faster for others. If you are reading to study 50-100 words is about right. If you want to find out how fast you read try the next brief task:

7.1b **Read for five minutes, count the words and divide by five.**

If you want to improve your reading speed then try to do ten minutes reading practice every day with your newspaper. You should notice an improvement within a very short time. Make sure that you:

- Read as fast as you can. Keep your eyes moving forward the whole time and don't let yourself back-track.

- Don't mouth the words silently to yourself.

Remember, it's sometimes difficult to read quickly and understand everything that you read. That's why some comprehension exercises have been included in this book. Look back at brief tasks 2.1b and 6.4a. Were you able to complete the tasks straight away or did you need to re-read the text?

If you find that you have to keep stopping when you read, because you are not familiar with the words, you may need to improve your vocabulary. Move on to the next Skill in this Section.

SKILL 2: | **VOCABULARY AND SPELLING**

Many people avoid writing because they are worried about their basic skills. Most of us haven't been taught grammar formally and, if we haven't practised our writing skills, are not very confident about spelling and punctuation.

The only way to improve your basic skills is to use them so Skills 2 and 3 in this Section consist of self-tests and tips to help you practise. If you are happy with all your basics move on to Skill 4.

Vocabulary
Often people find writing difficult because they can't think of the right word to use. Try the next brief task to test your vocabulary:

7.2a Here are ten words which are commonly found in health and safety documents at work. For each word, write down the meaning or a simpler alternative. Use a dictionary if you need to.

U006
E3

| data, fatality, flammable, hazard, incapacity, legislation, liability, notification, occurrences, practicable. |

If you didn't need to use a dictionary at all then you definitely haven't any vocabulary problems worth worrying about! Many people would find this task hard because the words used in official and legal documents are nearly always more difficult than they should be!

There are lots of different ways of increasing your vocabulary. Here are some tips to help you:

---

read widely: you will meet lots of new words used in different ways.

use new words: list words which are important to you and try to use them in conversation or writing.

look up words: when you meet a new word, look the word up in a dictionary and note down its meaning.

use a thesaurus: a thesaurus gives lots of alternative words which you could use instead of the one you are looking up. A good thesaurus is the New Collins Paperback Thesaurus in A-Z Form.

play games like Scrabble or complete a daily crossword puzzle: these are fun to do and, although you don't feel as if you are learning, you are!

Spelling can be a worry to many people. Try the next brief task:

7.2b Complete the following words, then check them in a dictionary.

---

a — — — ment (8 letters): a disagreement

ag — re — — i — — (10 letters): an assault or offensive behaviour

com — i — — — — (9 letters): a group appointed or elected for a special purpose

deve — — — (7 letters): to grow or advance

eff — — — — — (9 letters): well-organised

g — — ge (5 letters): a measure

i — — espon — — — — (13 letters): careless or unreliable

---

main — — — an — — (11 letters): keeping in good repair

o — — u — — ed (8 letters): having taken place or happened

sin — er — — — (9 letters): honestly (used to end letters to people whose names you know)

These are ten words which cause many people spelling problems. If you scored: 8-10 very good; 5-7 encouraging; 0-4 keep practising.

The secret of good spelling is to:

- **keep a small dictionary in your desk or bag at work:** use it to check spellings.

- **make your own personal dictionary:** buy a notebook. Write down any words that you need to use at work. Use a page for each word. Make sure that they are spelled correctly. Work on memorising a word by looking at it, covering it up, writing it again and checking it. Keep practising and leave longer and longer gaps between covering it up and writing it. Set yourself a target, for example five or ten words a week.

- **learn how to use a word processor:** these have automatic spelling check programs. However, you still need to know some basic spelling rules; for example, you may have used a word which is correctly spelt such as 'there' when really you should have used 'their'.

- **proofread all your writing:** you will get into the habit of checking for spelling mistakes.

SKILL 3: **GRAMMAR AND PUNCTUATION**

Grammar is a set of rules about language. Most of us know grammar although we can't formally describe it. It is important because it makes the meaning of your writing clear. It also matters when you complete job applications or write reports because mistakes might give the reader a poor impression of you. Generally, if something sounds right to you when you read it back to yourself it will probably sound right to the person who is reading it.

Punctuation marks help to make writing clear. They indicate where pauses would naturally be made if you read aloud.

7.3a List as many different ways of punctuating writing as you can think of.

You might have included:

Punctuation marks like: full stops (.), CAPITAL LETTERS, commas (,), colons (:) and semi-colons (;), apostrophes ('), brackets ( ), question marks (?), exclamation marks (!), hyphens (-), dashes (—), speech marks (' ').

Try the next brief task to test your own punctuation skills:

7.3b Each of the following words or phrases needs punctuation. Try to correct the errors.

> (a) T Harvey, the UN representative . . .
>
> (b) Lastly the report indicates . . .
>
> (c) A simple rule is to divide your report into three parts 1 introduction 2 main points 3 conclusions
>
> (d) The managers report . .
>
> (e) I don't know the answer, but I'll find out, he said.
>
> ANSWERS:
>
> (a) Full stops should really be used after initials and abbreviated words. Nowadays, they are often missed out. Full stops are also used to mark the end of a sentence. They should be followed by a capital letter.
>
> (b) Some words are nearly always used with commas: lastly, therefore, however, in fact. Commas indicate a short pause. They are also used to separate words in a list and to put extra bits in a sentence.

(c) Colons are used before a list. Semi-colons indicate a pause which is longer than a comma but shorter than a full stop. You could have corrected the sentence so that it reads '... parts: 1 introduction; 2 main points; 3 conclusions.' The sentence would still be correct if you used commas instead of semi-colons but there would have been less emphasis.

(d) The apostrophe is used to show who or what owns something. Managers should have read manager's. If there is more than one owner or the owner's name ends in an s then the apostrophe goes after the s. It is also used to show when a letter has been missed out e.g. it's instead of it is.

(e) You should have used speech marks (also called inverted commas) before and after what is actually said to indicate direct speech.

Punctuation tips:

- **use short sentences.** Sentences of more than about 25 words can be difficult to understand. If you break long sentences into shorter ones it will save you wasting time trying to decide between a colon and semi-colon.

- **keep paragraphs fairly short.** It will make your writing more readable.

- **check** your punctuation by reading your writing back to yourself. Does it sound right?

7.3c Read your company magazine or a newspaper. Use a highlighter pen to mark all the punctuation used in one or two articles. Think about why it has been used. Ask a friend or tutor for help if you're not sure.

SKILL 4: | DRAFTING AND EDITING

Once you have something down on paper, you have what is called the first or rough draft.

7.4a **1. Make some pattern notes about one of the following:**

> The staff canteen . . .
>
> Working hours . . .
>
> The advantages or disadvantages of joining a trade union . . .

2. Write a few sentences about each idea you had about the subject.

3. Put the ideas in a good order and write a rough draft.

You can now begin 'editing'. This means:

- changing some words so that they sound right for your reader.

- making it easier to understand – this might mean getting rid of unnecessary words.

- adding words and phrases.

- changing or developing ideas.

- changing the order.

- thinking about layout and presentation.

Here is an example of writing which is being edited:

> In some parts of the county local library's hold open learning materials. The librarian will ~~let you borrow and~~ help you choose packages, ~~and this will~~ *You may also* ~~enable you to~~ *borrow packs and* try out this type of learning.

7.4b **Look back at your first draft and edit it.**

You may need to write, edit and rewrite any writing several times. This is much easier and quicker to do if you are using a word processor. Once you have a draft that you are happy with, you can proofread it.

Proofreading is when you read word for word looking for spelling, punctuation and any factual mistakes.

Hints for proofreading:

- **get someone else to do it for you.** This is because when you read your own work you tend to read what you think it says rather than what you've actually written.

- **take a break before you start proofreading.** Then try to read as if you had never seen the piece of writing before.

- **look for common mistakes such as:**
  - spelling (check with a dictionary)
  - missing words
  - forgetting to use a capital letter
  - missing apostrophes.

SKILL 5: | REPORT WRITING |

At work you might be asked to write a short informal report. Before you start ask yourself two questions:

- why am I writing this report? (or, what do I want to happen when this report is read?)

- who am I writing it for?

This will help you decide on things like the tone of your writing. For example, you may want to write in a friendly way, particularly if you want to persuade your readers about something. If your readers are all experts, you will be able to use more technical terms.

Reports should have a clear beginning, a middle and an end.

The beginning should provide background information.

The middle should give the main points or describe your findings.

The end should give your conclusions and recommendations.

The first step is to get all your ideas down on paper. Try making some pattern notes *(see Section Two, Skill 4)*. Use the notes to help you decide how to start, what the main points are and how you are going to finish. Make a plan of what you are going to write.

Here is an example of notes for a report:

BRIGHT BROTHERS PLC

Report on the Service Provided by the Staff Canteen

T. Kitchen – Catering Manager

1. Introduction
- in response to increasing complaints
- carried out survey

2. Main points

2.1 present situation
- staff served at single sitting 12.30-1.30
- three course hot meal or choice from salad bar
- meals are subsidised

2.2 results from survey (40 questionnaires returned)
- some staff spend up to half lunch hour waiting to be served
- 50% staff complained about lack of variety
- 75% staff felt quality of food served was good
- all staff happy to pay more for improvements

2.3 catering staff felt pressure from 12.30-1.20 was intolerable

3. Conclusions and Recommendations

3.1 criticisms are justified

3.2 need to improve service or staff will lunch elsewhere
- introduce two lunch sittings
- introduce monthly menus with at least three choices of hot meals
- introduce second till to reduce queues.

When you start writing you may feel tempted to include everything! But if you want to be clear you must stick to the main points and be as brief as possible. Don't use long, unnecessary phrases.

7.5a **Replace the following phrases with one or two words.**

'at this point in time'	'for the reason that'
'be in a position to'	'in the event that'
'in connection with'	

The words that you could have used are:

now	we	can	about	because	if

Check your own reports with this self-check:

SELF-CHECK **Report-writing**

Have you...	Yes	No
● used headings to help people understand what you are writing?	☐	☐
● made the report good to look at and neat and tidy?	☐	☐
● used facts and figures and kept to the point?	☐	☐
● said what you wanted to say?	☐	☐
● proofread the final draft?	☐	☐
● always given the word or title in full before using an abbreviation, e.g. Work's Warehouse Department (WWD)?	☐	☐
● used short words rather than long, e.g. use rather than utilise?	☐	☐
● kept your sentences short?	☐	☐

WORK-RELATED ACTIVITIES

7A. Use the rough notes and drafts you prepared for brief tasks 7.3a and b and write a short report on that topic. Make sure you produce several paragraphs of writing (up to one side of type). Use the self-check on page 100 to assess your own report.

U009
E1 or E2

7B. If you have to write a report at work, keep copies of your rough notes, drafts and final report.

U009
E1

You could choose to do activity 8A on page 115 instead.

SUPERVISING OTHERS

Lots of people don't bother to apply for promotion because they worry about dealing with people they have been working with, or handling the paperwork or coping with new responsibilities. Others do the job for a few weeks and decide it '. . . just isn't for them'.

We've seen in earlier Sections of this book that jobs are becoming more complex and everyone has to take more responsibility at work. For example, anyone who works in a team may have to coach others or give instructions. Everyone has responsibilities for health and safety. So this Section is not just for supervisors.

However, if you are thinking about promotion sometime in the future you might want to practise the skills now. If you are a supervisor already you may want to review your current performance and see if you learn anything new.

This Section will help you to:

- be better at giving instructions and setting standards
- demonstrate good coaching skills
- be better at identifying health and safety problems
- manage work-related paperwork
- build good working relationships.

SKILL 1:

GIVING INSTRUCTIONS AND SETTING STANDARDS

The supervisor's job is to allocate work, give instructions, report back to senior management and to deal with situations as they arise.

One of the hardest jobs for anyone who has just been promoted is to give instructions. Telling people what to do isn't as simple as it sounds. See how good you are by trying the next brief task.

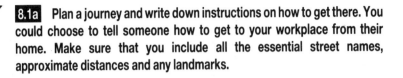

8.1a Plan a journey and write down instructions on how to get there. You could choose to tell someone how to get to your workplace from their home. Make sure that you include all the essential street names, approximate distances and any landmarks.

If you want to practise writing instructions you could make up sets of instructions for any tasks. Start with something fairly simple like making a cup of tea, using a coffee machine or using a photocopier at work. Ask someone who has not carried out this task before to follow your instructions. Use the self-check below to see how good your instructions are:

SELF-CHECK   **Writing instructions**

Was the person carrying out the instructions:	Yes	No
• able to complete the task without asking for more information?	☐	☐
Did they find that the instructions were:		
• easy to follow?	☐	☐
• in the right order?	☐	☐

If you answered 'no' to any of these questions, write the instructions out again and make them clearer.

Here are some tips for writing instructions:

- make a list of key points and check that they are in a sensible order.

- consider who you are instructing. A more experienced member of staff will need less detail than a trainee.

- identify any problems which might arise and make sure the other person knows how to deal with them.

As a supervisor you are, or will be, accountable for the quality of work in your area. This means that you will have to make sure that every task is carried out consistently to a standard which meets the needs of your organisation. If you are going to achieve this you need to set clear standards.

Writing standards sounds more difficult that it actually is. We all have standards although yours may be higher or lower than someone else's!

8.1b Compare the standards below with your own, and tick whether yours are higher, lower or the same.

My standards are: Higher Lower Same	Personal quality standards
	1. Exercise at least three times a week.
	2. Write thank-you letters within one week of receiving a present.
	3. Clean car every two weeks.
	4. Never arrive late for work.
	5. Return all telephone calls within 12 hours.

These standards are very clear. Your own may be very different, for example, lots of people rarely clean their cars! Work standards will depend on what your customers want and expect.

Look at these examples of quality standards:

- Upon entering the restaurant, customers are greeted within 30 seconds.

- These toilets are checked by our staff once every hour.

- Customers receive water refills without having to ask.

- All patients are seen by the doctor within 30 minutes of their appointment time.

8.1c Try writing a few quality standards for your own job or write a set of personal standards.

U009
E1

SKILL 2: | COACHING SKILLS

People who carry out coaching need to be trained themselves to learn the teaching skills needed. It is possible to be the best welder in the firm but to be absolutely hopeless at teaching other people new skills!

If you are responsible for coaching you will need to coach:

- new members of staff.

- when you change work practices or introduce new equipment.

- to help staff solve work problems.

- to help staff who make mistakes.

- to help improve the performance of staff (this could mean coaching when someone does a task well, so your team understands why).

If you do need to coach staff use the following self-check to help:

SELF-CHECK Coaching skills

Before coaching, have you ...	Yes	No
• broken down the task into simple stages and identified the key teaching points at each stage?	☐	☐
• briefed the trainee so they know what is going to happen and what is expected of them?	☐	☐

During coaching, did you ...	Yes	No
• carefully demonstrate the task, explaining the key teaching points?	☐	☐
• ask the trainee to carry out the task?	☐	☐
• ask the trainee questions to check their understanding?	☐	☐
• listen carefully and give a positive response?	☐	☐
• provide objective feedback to the trainee?	☐	☐

After coaching, did you ...

	Yes	No
• sit down with the trainee and review the coaching:		
– did the trainee learn how to do the task?	☐	☐
– could you have explained it differently?	☐	☐
• discuss the next step with the trainee?	☐	☐

SKILL 3:

HEALTH AND SAFETY

All health and safety laws are designed to reduce the high number of work-related deaths and injuries.

Did you know ...

that every year over 500 people die at work and several hundred thousand lose time through illness and injury?

Anyone who works needs to be able to:

- identify risks at work.
- try to reduce them by developing a sense of safety.
- follow correct procedures and take protective measures.
- report any problems to managers and make sure that they are put right.

In addition to this, supervisors have specific responsibilities and may have to draw up safety checklists and instruct staff.

8.3a Talk about health and safety with your workmates and make a list of some of the problems people have had in the past year.

Unless you are all very health and safety conscious, you might have included:

- trips and falls
- back problems
- food poisoning
- electric shocks
- burns and cuts

- breathing problems or asthma
- accidents with machinery
- stress-related illnesses
- skin problems or eye irritation.

You probably found that health and safety problems are more common at work than you thought!

All of these problems can be avoided. Use the following self-check to see if you follow safe working practices. Remember that if you are a supervisor you should ensure that your staff can answer 'yes' to each of these points.

SELF-CHECK **Safe working practices**

Do you...	Yes	No
• understand your organisation's health and safety policy?	☐	☐
• know about any specific arrangements for coping with particular hazards in your department or section?	☐	☐
• know about fire procedures?	☐	☐
• ask for safety checklists and training when you think they are needed?	☐	☐

	Yes	No
• look for things which are unsafe or potentially unsafe?	☐	☐
• keep your work area clean and tidy? (to reduce the risk of accidents from falling and tripping)	☐	☐
• follow instructions for operating machinery?	☐	☐
• always use, or wear, protective equipment when appropriate?	☐	☐
• know where fire fighting and first aid equipment is kept?	☐	☐
• use correct lifting techniques?	☐	☐
• always report accidents?	☐	☐

If you answered 'yes' to all these questions, good. If you said 'no' then discuss the issue with your line manager and/or shop steward.

8.3b **Find at least five examples of health and safety notices in your workplace (e.g. warning signs, fire action instructions, fire extinguisher codes, first and emergency aid notices). Make sure you understand them.**

An important part of health and safety law are the Control of Substances Hazardous to Health (COSHH) regulations. These apply to all workplaces. They require every employer to carry out an assessment of the risks arising from exposure to any hazardous substances in the workplace.

Hazardous substances have to be labelled by law:

very toxic	toxic	corrosive	harmful	irritant

The labels must have hazard warning symbols and should tell you:

- What the hazards are, e.g.

  – highly flammable   – poisonous or toxic

  – hazardous (e.g. irritant) ✖

- Advice on how to reduce the risks, e.g.

  - keep away from heat, or

  - use gloves, eye protection and protective clothing when handling this material.

There should also be a Hazard Data Sheet supplied with each product. This will give details of:

- hazards
- precautions
- storage
- first aid measures
- action in case of spillage.

8.3c Make a list of all the substances that you come into contact with at work.

1. Check to see if there is a hazard warning sign. If there is find out what it means.
2. Read the label to see what the hazards are. Write them down.
3. Write down any precautions which need to be taken before using the substance.
4. Ask your manager if there is a Hazard Data Sheet. Write down any other requirements for the safe use of each product.
5. Check both the label and Hazard Data Sheet to see if there are any special instructions for storage or procedures to be taken in case of emergency.
6. Write up your notes neatly.

U006	U007	U010
E1 & E2	E1	E2

This will take you about one hour but it depends on how many hazardous substances are used in your workplace!

SKILL 4: **DEALING WITH PAPERWORK**

It can be a shock to a new supervisor to see the amount of paperwork that needs to be dealt with in a day.

8.4a Make a list of the paperwork which you or your supervisor has to send and receive.

Estimate how long you or your supervisor spend writing in your job – you may be surprised!

Supervisors normally have to send and receive instructions, forms, letters, messages, reports, notes and memos. You may have even more on your list. Most of these have already been discussed (see pages 47, 80, 82 and 98) so this section will concentrate on memos and accident reports.

Memos

It's worth getting into the habit of sending memos to pass on information. Memo is an abbreviation of Memorandum. Memos are a quick and efficient way of sending messages at work. They can be used to:

- send an instruction
- put forward suggestions
- provide information
- to express a point of view.

A dictionary definition of memorandum is *'a note to help memory'*, so they should be short and to the point. Memos provide a permanent record and should always be kept. Here is an example:

MEMO

To: All Supervisors

From: B. Ware, Safety Officer

Date: 18 September 1991

FIRE DRILL

Please ensure that all your staff are reminded about fire procedures. There will be a fire drill sometime during the next month.

Some organisations have a special form, like the one below:

BRIGHT BROTHERS PLC:

Memorandum

TO:..DEPARTMENT: ....

FROM:...DEPARTMENT: ....

DATE: ....

SUBJECT: ....

MESSAGE: ....

....

....

....

....

COPIES TO: ....

....

25

U008
E1 & E2

8.4b Draft a memorandum. Make up the information. You could choose one of the following sentences to get you started:

'Following our recent discussions about . . .'

'I will be unable to attend . . .'

'I believe we could make cost savings by . . .'

'I would like to put forward the following idea to the Staff Suggestion Scheme . . .'

Accident reports

Most people will have to complete an accident report at some time during their working life. The law is very strict about this so that:

● problems can be investigated to prevent the accident happening again.

● there is an accurate record in case of any legal action.

● information on accidents and injuries can be collected and used to identify accident trends.

You will need to answer five key questions:

● **when?** . . . give the date and time of the accident.

● **who?** . . . give your name and the names of any witnesses.

● **where?** . . . say exactly where the accident happened.

● **what?** . . . explain exactly what happened.

● **why?** . . . say why you think the accident happened.

8.4c Use the following information to fill out the accident form on the right. Make up any other information needed to complete the form.

> You are a catering assistant and slipped on some oil spilt near the deep fat fryer. As you fell, your hand hit a pan handle which was sticking out over the edge of the hob. The pan was knocked off and you were covered by hot soup. Luckily you were wearing protective clothing but one of your hands was badly burnt and you were taken to the nearest hospital casualty department. There have been staff shortages in the kitchen recently. The standard of cleanliness has suffered and you know the floor had not been cleaned for two days.
>
> You could use an accident form from your workplace instead and write up an example of an accident that you know about.
>
> U008
> E1 & E2

BRIGHT BROTHERS PLC

Accident on Duty-Report by Injured Employee

I wish to report an accident on duty. Details of the accident are given below and it has been recorded in the Accident Book.

Date of Accident .... Time ....Place ....

What was the accident and how did it happen? ....

....

....

....

....

Type of injury and part of body affected ....

....

Names and addresses of witnesses ....

....

....

What protective clothing were you wearing? ....

....

Signature...Job Title ....

Name...Date ....
(block letters)

SKILL 5: | DEVELOPING GOOD WORKING RELATIONSHIPS

Most of the problems which people have at work are caused by other people. If you're not sure whether you agree with this statement, try the next brief task:

8.5a Think about a recent problem you had at work. Was this problem caused by 'people' or 'machines' or by both?

You probably answered people or both. A supervisor needs to remember that people are the organisation's greatest asset and should be handled with care. Good working relationships are built on mutual respect and trust.

Use the following self-check to see if you are building good working relationships.

SELF-CHECK **Developing good working relationships**

Do you...	Yes	No
• let staff know what is happening and why?	☐	☐
• make sure that staff know what you want from them?	☐	☐
• recognise their skills and talents		
– by listening to, and asking for, their suggestions?	☐	☐
– by praising good performance?	☐	☐
• help staff overcome their weaknesses		
– by giving honest feedback?	☐	☐
– coaching to remedy mistakes?	☐	☐
• lead by example?	☐	☐
• help out when your staff are under pressure to meet deadlines?	☐	☐

	Yes	No
• make sure that you are seen to be fair		
– by ensuring that you don't have favourites?	☐	☐
– by taking firm action when you identify poor performance from any member of staff?	☐	☐
• show an interest in your staff as people?	☐	☐
• give advice and support when asked?	☐	☐

If you are thinking about applying for a supervisory post why not discuss it with your boss or line manager or the person responsible for training?

WORK-RELATED ACTIVITIES

8A. Walk around your workplace and look for things which are unsafe or potentially unsafe. Jot these down.

Use your notes to make a written report outlining the problems and making recommendations for improvements.

Look back to Section Seven, Skill 5 for help with report writing and use the self-check to review your final draft.

U009
E1

If you prefer, you could make a verbal report. Look back to page 64 to remind yourself of the skills needed when giving a short talk.

U010
E1

8B. If you deal with paperwork as part of your job, keep copies as evidence of your competence.

U009
E1

If you give instructions and/or have discussions with a colleague which involve obtaining information by asking questions, tape some of your conversations.

U010
E1 and/or E2

MORE ABOUT THE CITY AND GUILDS 3793 CERTIFICATE IN COMMUNICATION SKILLS (WORDPOWER)

This book will help you work towards this Certificate. The Certificate has four levels: Foundation, Stage 1, Stage 2 and Stage 3. This book generally covers the listening, speaking, reading and writing skills that you need for work and training at Stage 1, although some of the topics and tasks are relevant to Stages 2 and 3. If you want to get a qualification it really is best to contact a tutor in a centre offering the Certificate before you start. They will be able to give you specific advice about assessment which is suited to your own situation. You will also get advice about which level of the Certificate is best for you to aim for.

The Certificate is made up of **units.** Each unit is made up of **two, three or four elements** and each element is made up of between **two and five tasks.** You need to collect evidence that you have completed every task to the required standard. The chart below tells you more about the units, elements and tasks at Stage 1 and gives you some ideas for collecting evidence for assessment at this level. Whatever level you work towards, a tutor or trainer will need to make sure that your work is of a high enough standard for the Certificate. They may also ask you to produce some additional work.

Unit	Element	How you can show evidence that you have these skills
Unit 006 is about reading text	1: getting the main idea	Complete four of the following tasks: 2.1b, 5.2b, 6.3a, 6.4a, 6B or be able to extract information from four pieces of paperwork e.g. a manual, a policy, an advertisement and a newspaper.

Unit	Element	How you can show evidence that you have these skills
	2: reading instructions	Complete tasks 3.1b and 8.3c or show that you can follow any two sets of instructions at work e.g. operate machines, use a photocopier.
	3: using reference material	Complete two of the following tasks: 1.1a, 4.1b, 5.2b, 7.2a or 7.2b.
Unit 007 is about under-standing graphical material	1: understanding signs and labels	You should complete 8.3b. You could also complete 8.3c.
	2: using a map or plan	You should complete 8.1a and plan two other journeys using an A-Z, road map etc. These could be your trip to the library for task 4.1c or to the Jobcentre for 5.2b.
	3: getting information from tables	You should complete 4.3a.
Unit 008 is about forms	1: understanding forms 2: filling in forms	Complete at least two of the following: 3.3c, 3.5a, 5B, 6B, 8.4b, 8.4c. These cover elements 1 and 2.
Unit 009 is about writing	1: writing reports, letters, notes and other messages	Complete at least four of the following: 1B, 2.4b, 2B, 5.2b, 5A, 5B, 6.3a, 6A, 6B, 7B, 8.1c, 8.3c, 8A, 8B.
	2. writing about ideas and experiences	Complete at least three of the following: 1.5c, 2.3a, 3A, 7A.
Unit 010 is about talking to one other person	1: giving information to someone face-to-face or on the telephone	Complete at least three of the following tasks: 2A, 3B, 5B, 6B, 8A, 8B.
	2: asking someone for information face-to-face or on the telephone	Complete at least three of the folowing: 1.1b, 1.3b, 2.1b, 3.1b, 3B, 4.1c, 5.2b, 5.2c, 6B, 8.3c, 8B.

Unit	Element	How you can show evidence that you have these skills
	3: making conversation with a stranger	You can use any two of the tasks listed for Elements 1, 2 and 4 of this Unit as long as you don't know the person.
	4: reassuring someone who is in an unfamiliar situation	You could complete activity 1A and provide evidence of one other example e.g. helping someone who is worried about a change of job, advising a new member of your team at work.
Unit 011 is about talking to more than one person	1: performing introductions and farewells	Get somone to witness you doing this at a meeting, when you meet some new people, or when you introduce someone to other members of your team. You need two examples.
	2: giving information to more than one person	Complete two of the following: 1B, 2B, 4A, 4B, 5B.
Unit 012 is about getting information from audio-visual material	1: getting information from a talk or lecture	Ask questions at a staff meeting or briefing and complete 4C. You need two examples.
	2. getting information from TV, video or radio	Complete two of the following: 2.4a, 4.4a, 4C.

Don't forget that you could choose your own tasks to prove that you have the skills described in the elements. Do get advice from a trainer or tutor before you start.

GLOSSARY OF TERMS

Bar charts, pie charts and graphs: are ways of presenting information. A bar chart looks like lots of bars all standing together; a pie chart like a pie cut into portions; graphs are lines on a chart showing the relationship between two things.

Brainstorming: is a way of coming up with a lot of ideas in a short time. People make suggestions which are written up on a board or flip chart.

Career Development Loans: are loans of between £300 and £5,000 towards the cost of training. They are available to anyone, whether unemployed or employed, aged 18 or over.

Coaching: helps people improve their performance. The trainee is given planned tasks and counselling by his or her supervisor.

COSHH: is the abbreviation for Control of Substances Hazardous to Health. They are health and safety regulations.

Contact List: is a list of the names and addresses of people who are relevant to your work and/or who can provide you with information.

Distance learning: is individual home study like a correspondence course.

Flip charts: are large sheets of white paper fixed to a frame. The sheets can be flipped over easily. They are used a lot for training and presentations.

Improvement Group: see Quality Circle.

Multi-Skilling: is the process by which employees are trained to carry out a range of diffferent jobs.

Open Learning: is really supported self-study. You learn at your own pace and at a time and place to suit you.

Overhead projectors (OHPs): are machines which project images on to a screen. Notes and pictures can be written, drawn or photocopied onto a plastic sheet (called a transparency) and placed on the OHP. When the machine is switched on the notes are projected on to the screen.

Performance Criteria: are the standards set for achieving qualifications.

Portfolio: is a collection of work showing evidence of achievements.

Quality Circle: These are sometimes called 'improvement groups'. Groups of employees meet regularly to identify, analyse and solve work-related problems.

Single European Market: in 1992 all restrictions on internal trade within the European Economic Community (EEC) will be lifted. This will increase competition between companies.

Team Briefings: are a structured process of briefing whereby senior managers brief middle managers, who in turn brief junior managers, who brief supervisors, who then brief their work teams. They are usually based on a model provided by the Industrial Society.

Training Vouchers: these are sometimes called 'training credits'. They are grants which can be used to pay for training or training advice. They may be available if you are under 18, unemployed or low paid. They are only available in some parts of the country.

WHERE TO FIND OUT MORE

You could contact any of the organisations below asking for further information. For tips on writing letters see page 84.

Adult Literacy and Basic Skills Unit: publish useful workpacks called *'The Spelling Pack'* and *'The Numeracy Pack'*. Ask for a copy of their publications catalogue. Employers and tutors can also ask for advice on any aspect of basic skills training.

Adult Literacy & Basic Skills Unit, Kingsbourne House, 229-231 High Holborn, London WC1V 7DA.

Careers Service: for advice on training and employment opportunities. They work mainly with younger people but they will be able to tell you about any Education Guidance Services for Adults.

The address and telephone number will be in the telephone book under Careers Service or the local education authority.

City and Guilds of London Institute: for more about the Certificate in Communication Skills.

Division 31, 46 Britannia Street, London WC1X 9RG.

Health and Safety Executive (HSE): for information about health and safety and free leaflets contact one of the HSE public enquiry points between 10am and 3pm Monday to Friday.

Baynards House, 1 Chepstow Place, Westbourne Grove, London W2 4FT. Tel: 071 221 0870

Broad Lane, Sheffield S3 7HQ. Tel: 0742 752539

Industrial Society: works mainly with employers but has useful books about team briefings, quality circles and general communication skills for supervisors. Ask for a copy of their Publications Catalogue.

Sales Unit (Publications), The Industrial Society, Quadrant Court, 49 Calthorpe Road, Edgbaston, Birmingham B15 1TH.

Jobcentres: can tell you more about training opportunities and benefits if you are unemployed; Training and Enterprise Councils (TECs), or local enterprise companies in Scotland; Training Access Points (TAPs) and Career Development

Loans (CDLs). You will find the telephone number of your local Jobcentre in the telephone book under 'J'.

Open College: provides a range of open learning courses. Ask for more details.

The Open College, Freepost, PO Box 35, Abingdon OX14 3BR

Royal Society for the Prevention of Accidents: for more about Health and Safety.

RoSPA, Cannon House, The Priory, Queensway, Birmingham B4 6BS.

Trades Union Congress (TUC): will give you more information about trade unions and health and safety.

TUC, Congress House, Great Russell Street, London WC1B 3LS.

You could also read the following books:

Essentials of Health and Safety at Work, published by HMSO, for more about health and safety.

Improve your People Skills, by Peter Honey, published by IPM, for more about understanding behaviour at work.

In the Know, by Martin Good and Christopher South, published by BBC Books and *Mastering Study Skills* by R. Freeman, published by MacMillan, for more about learning and studying.

Quality at Work, by D. Bone and R. Griggs, published by Kogan Page, for an introduction to quality issues.

Supervision, by Mike Savedra and John Hawthorn, published by MacMillan. A self-study book.

The Penguin WordMaster Dictionary, by Martin Manser and Nigel Turton, published by Penguin Books, for more about words.

Step up to Wordpower, by Carolyn Kewley and Angela Lee, published by BBC Books for more about reading, writing, talking and listening.

Trainers and tutors offering the City and Guilds certificate in Communication Skills will find the two workpacks, *Crediting Communication Skills* – Foundation and Stage 1 and *Crediting Communication Skills* – Stages 2 and 3, invaluable. They are available from the Adult Literacy and Basic Skills Unit, address above.

INDEX

INDEX

You may be interested in the following titles published by BBC Books:

Step up to Wordpower – A Practical Start to Improve Communication Skills, Carolyn Kewley and Angela Lee.

A Way with Numbers – A Practical Start to Improve Numeracy Skills, Terry Riley.

Finding the Right Job, Anne Segall and William Grierson.

Spelling it Out, Rhiannedd Pratley.

OK2 – Talk Feelings, Dr Jenny Cozens.

Use Your Head, Tony Buzan.

Use Your Memory, Tony Buzan.

Women Mean Business, Caroline Bamford and Catherine McCarthy.

Assertiveness – The Right to be You, Clare Walmsley.